THE GUN CONTROL DEBATE

FROM CLASSROOMS TO CONGRESS

By Lianna Tatman

Portions of this book originally appeared in *Gun Control* by Jenny MacKay.

LUCENT PRESS

Published in 2020 by
Lucent Press, an Imprint of Greenhaven Publishing, LLC
353 3rd Avenue
Suite 255
New York, NY 10010

Designer: Deanna Paternostro
Editor: Jennifer Lombardo

Library of Congress Cataloging-in-Publication Data

Names: Tatman, Lianna, author.
Title: The gun control debate : from classrooms to Congress / Lianna Tatman.
Description: New York : Lucent Press, 2020. | Series: Hot topics | Includes
  bibliographical references and index.
Identifiers: LCCN 2019002532 (print) | LCCN 2019005225 (ebook) | ISBN
  9781534567627 (eBook) | ISBN 9781534567610 (pbk. book) | ISBN
  9781534566996 (library bound book)
Subjects: LCSH: Firearms–Law and legislation–United States–Juvenile
  literature. | Gun control–United States–Juvenile literature.
Classification: LCC KF3941 (ebook) | LCC KF3941 .T38 2020 (print) | DDC
  363.330973–dc23
LC record available at https://lccn.loc.gov/2019002532

Printed in the United States of America

CPSIA compliance information: Batch #BS19KL: For further information contact Greenhaven Publishing LLC, New York,
New York at 1-844-317-7404.

Please visit our website, www.greenhavenpublishing.com. For a free color catalog of all our
high-quality books, call toll free 1-844-317-7404 or fax 1-844-317-7405.

CONTENTS

FOREWORD 4

INTRODUCTION 6
The Parkland Massacre

CHAPTER 1 9
America's History with Firearms

CHAPTER 2 26
Guns and the Law

CHAPTER 3 43
The Gun Control Side

CHAPTER 4 64
The Gun Rights Side

CHAPTER 5 77
The Debate Is Ongoing

NOTES 88
DISCUSSION QUESTIONS 94
ORGANIZATIONS TO CONTACT 96
FOR MORE INFORMATION 98
INDEX 100
PICTURE CREDITS 103
ABOUT THE AUTHOR 104

Adolescence is a time when many people begin to take notice of the world around them. News channels, blogs, and talk radio shows are constantly promoting one view or another; very few are unbiased. Young people also hear conflicting information from parents, friends, teachers, and acquaintances. Often, they will hear only one side of an issue or be given flawed information. People who are trying to support a particular viewpoint may cite inaccurate facts and statistics on their blogs, and news programs present many conflicting views of important issues in our society. In a world where it seems everyone has a platform to share their thoughts, it can be difficult to find unbiased, accurate information about important issues.

It is not only facts that are important. In blog posts, in comments on online videos, and on talk shows, people will share opinions that are not necessarily true or false, but can still have a strong impact. For example, many young people struggle with their body image. Seeing or hearing negative comments about particular body types online can have a huge effect on the way someone views himself or herself and may lead to depression and anxiety. Although it is important not to keep information hidden from young people under the guise of protecting them, it is equally important to offer encouragement on issues that affect their mental health.

The titles in the Hot Topics series provide readers with different viewpoints on important issues in today's society. Many of these issues, such as gang violence and gun control laws, are of immediate concern to young people. This series aims to give readers factual context on these crucial topics in a way that lets them form their own opinions. The facts presented throughout also serve to empower readers to help themselves or support people they know who are struggling with many of the challenges adolescents face today. Although negative viewpoints are not ignored or downplayed, this series allows young people to see that the challenges they face are not insurmountable. As increasing numbers of young adults join political debates, especially regarding gun violence, learning the facts as well as the views of others will help them decide where they stand—and understand what they are fighting for.

Quotes encompassing all viewpoints are presented and cited so readers can trace them back to their original source, verifying for themselves whether the information comes from a reputable place. Additional books and websites are listed, giving readers a starting point from which to continue their own research. Chapter questions encourage discussion, allowing young people to hear and understand their classmates' points of view as they further solidify their own. Full-color photographs and enlightening charts provide a deeper understanding of the topics at hand. All of these features augment the informative text, helping young people understand the world they live in and formulate their own opinions concerning the best way they can improve it.

The Parkland Massacre

On February 14, 2018, at Marjory Stoneman Douglas High School in Parkland, Florida, former student Nikolas Cruz opened fire on students and faculty members. Twelve were murdered in the building, two were killed outside, one victim died in the street, and two succumbed to their injuries in the local hospital. Melissa Falkowski, a teacher at the high school, stated that another faculty member alerted her that it was a code red—an active shooter—as she was leading her students out of the building after Cruz pulled a fire alarm. She led them back into her classroom, locked the door, and hid with them for 40 minutes. She credited her survival, and that of her students, to the recent active shooter drills and training she received. Unfortunately, she said, it was not enough: "We did everything that we were supposed to do. Broward County Schools has prepared us for this situation and still to have so many casualties, at least for me, it's very emotional. Because I feel today like our government, our country has failed us and failed our kids and didn't keep us safe."[1]

How did Parkland—voted the safest city in Florida in 2017—become the setting for one of the deadliest mass shootings in recent U.S. history? More importantly, can this be prevented from happening in the future? School shootings are horrifying events American families have come to fear. At the heart of the issue is whether or not the problem of interpersonal violence can be solved by eliminating guns from society. Every time another school shooting occurs, both sides of the gun control debate seize on it as an example of why their position is right. After the

After the Parkland shooting, some surviving students, such as Emma González and David Hogg, became internationally known for speaking out about gun control.

tragedy, gun control activists maintained that it is far too easy for American children and teens to get their hands on firearms, making tragedies such as the Parkland shooting the inevitable outcome. Gun rights activists defended the position that the blame in such tragedies belongs solely to the shooter who uses the gun to carry out the crime.

Gun control advocates used the case to back their claims that the nation needs more effective laws regulating who can purchase a firearm. Cruz purchased the gun—a type called an AR-15—because it was "cool looking."[2] The state of Florida did not require fingerprints, a permit, or a waiting period to purchase a gun. The only requirements were that the buyer be over the age of 18 and submit to a background check to verify that they did not have a criminal record. In response to the Parkland shooting, Florida governor Rick Scott signed a gun control law that adjusted the age requirement to 21 years and implemented a three-day waiting period before the buyer can take their weapon home. This gun control law is the only successful gun control measure the state of Florida has seen in 20 years.

Those in favor of gun rights have responded as well. As of early 2019, only one state aside from Florida has passed any meaningful firearm reform since the Parkland shooting, and the National Rifle Association (NRA) is challenging Florida's bill in court. One of the primary arguments in favor of gun rights is that the people committing these crimes are already breaking the law because regardless of how someone acquired a gun, using it to commit murder is illegal. Therefore, they say, passing new gun control laws will not matter because a criminal will simply break those too.

While many of the students from Marjory Stoneman Douglas High School have been advocating for stricter gun control, not all of them are. Kyle Kashuv, who was 16 years old when he survived the Parkland shooting, is a staunch supporter of gun rights, stating that the Second Amendment—the right to bear arms—protects all the other amendments. Kyle and his classmates are now pivotal players in the ongoing debate between gun control and gun rights.

America's History with Firearms

In many Western nations, gun ownership is strictly regulated, and most average citizens do not own any guns. There is little pushback on the restriction of gun ownership because guns are not considered to be culturally significant the way they are in the United States. In the United Kingdom (UK), even the average police officer does not carry a firearm, although some do.

In the United States, however, guns have been linked to freedom, democracy, expansion, and growth in many citizens' minds for hundreds of years. For early Americans, firearms were essential tools for hunting and self-defense, but even before the United States became a country, American colonists were

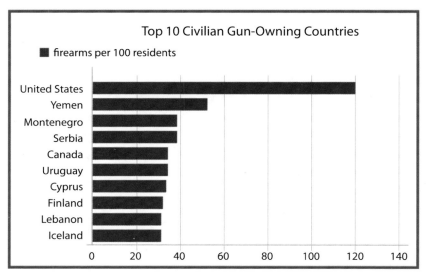

The United States has the most guns per person out of any country in the world, as this information from the BBC shows.

sometimes at odds about whether guns were a good idea in the new land. The debate about these deadly weapons is deeply rooted in American history and culture.

The Origin of Guns

Firearms existed long before the first Europeans came to America. Historians believe firepower originated in about AD 300 in ancient China. Chinese inventors wrote about the discovery of a powder that exploded when exposed to flame. Recipes for making the powder eventually migrated to Europe during trading expeditions. In the mid-1200s, Europeans experimented with new ways to use the explosive powder, and by the 1340s, the cannon had become a powerful weapon.

Cannons were standard wartime weapons in the Middle Ages, but their size and weight limited their usefulness. In the late 1300s, people in Italy and England invented miniature, handheld cannons which became known as "hand guns." These worked by the same principle as cannons, requiring the user to add gunpowder to the barrel and insert a small lead ball. The powder in the gun had to be ignited by a match or a small fuse before the bullet would be discharged. Using a match meant the shooter had only one hand free to steady the gun. Using a fuse freed both hands so the shooter could stabilize the weapon,

*Cannons were a useful tool for defending cities,
but they were too heavy to be moved quickly.*

but fuses caused a delay between lighting the flame and firing the shot, and in rainy weather, fuses could be extinguished before the gun fired. Early handguns were difficult to use, hard to aim, and limited in range. They could shoot a bullet only 30 to 40 yards (27 to 37 m).

In the 1400s, guns were modernized with a spring-loaded mechanism to strike a piece of flint against a strip of iron. The movement shaved off a speck of flaming iron that dropped into the gunpowder. Guns could now be shot with a tug of a spring-loaded trigger. Both hands steadied the weapon, which made it more accurate. Bullets were expelled with enough force to pierce not only armor but also animal hide. Guns became popular in Europe for battles, self-defense, and hunting. In 1690, the British began mass-producing various closely related muskets patterned after an original model called the Brown Bess. These became the standard guns used by the British army for the next century. According to sociologist Gregg Lee Carter, "The efficient use of the Bess, in fact, put the British regulars among the most effective and feared troops of the period."[3]

The effectiveness and power of guns made them popular but controversial among Europeans, especially the British, who had the world's most sophisticated and powerful national military. Some British subjects were concerned about the killing ability of guns, but others saw guns as necessary tools to protect themselves from the army of any king who might want to control them. In 1689, the British passed the English Bill of Rights, which granted the people certain freedoms and protections. One of those protections read, "Subjects which are Protestants may have arms for their defense suitable to their conditions, and as allowed by law."[4] An armed citizenry would be able to stand up to foes, even a tyrannical king.

BYOG (Bring Your Own Gun)

The British belief in an armed citizenry spread overseas to the new British colonies in North America. Guns were necessary tools in the new land, used for hunting and self-defense. The colonists, like the citizens of their homeland, were wary of a powerful king who could command an armed military to control the people. They eventually faced off against exactly such a ruler when they united against King George III in the 1770s, declared themselves an independent country, and went to war against Britain's powerful military. The newborn United States of America had no money for a large national army. Its fighting forces during the American Revolution consisted largely of a militia of private citizens who brought their guns from home.

Because the American colonies won their independence from Great Britain by creating a militia of ordinary citizens who owned guns, the concept of freedom became inseparably linked with gun ownership in American culture.

The untrained militia was poorly suited for war. Most militia soldiers had little or no formal battle training, and although they had guns, many were not experts at using them. Nevertheless, after years of vicious fighting, the United States won its freedom from Britain. It then faced the task of establishing a government and a constitution, and one of the most pressing controversies was what to do about national defense. Some citizens thought guns were dangerous in the hands of untrained users and best suited for professional soldiers in a national army. Others believed allowing private citizens to own firearms guaranteed that the new government could never overpower its people. In 1791, the Bill of Rights was ratified. This is a list of amendments that clarified the original U.S. Constitution. After the American Revolution, many citizens feared a government that would try to control them, so they pushed for what became the Second Amendment. The amendment is worded, "A well regulated Militia, being necessary to the security of a free State, the right of the people to keep and bear Arms, shall not be infringed."[5] Under the protection of this Second Amendment, American citizens have practiced their right to make, buy, and use firearms ever since.

DEBATED, BUT STILL RELEVANT

"Undoubtedly some think that the Second Amendment is outmoded in a society where our standing army is the pride of our nation ... What is not debatable is that it is not the role of this court to pronounce the Second Amendment extinct."

—Antonin Scalia, U.S. Supreme Court Justice

Quoted in Bill Mears, "High Court Strikes Down Gun Ban," CNN, June 26, 2008. www.cnn.com/2008/US/06/26/scotus.guns/.

Early Gun Laws

The Second Amendment right to keep and bear arms, including guns, is a fundamental part of American history, but it has also caused considerable problems for the American people. Gun manufacturers continually make weapons even more accurate and lethal. Rampant gun violence has marked several famous eras of U.S. development and has led to numerous calls for better regulation of firearms.

As the United States expanded westward throughout the 1800s, the western frontier became a vast area of cattle ranches, scattered towns, and widespread lawlessness. Guns accompanied cowboys and outlaws into this Wild West, especially the popular six-shooter—a pistol that held six bullets in a revolving ammunition cartridge. Many westerners had holsters attached to their belts for carrying two such handguns with them at all times. Arguments that erupted on streets or in saloons sometimes ended in dangerous exchanges of gunfire.

Many citizens of the Wild West demanded regulation of firearms, at least within towns and cities. Some towns were created mainly so the citizens could form a local governing body with the authority to forbid people to carry or shoot guns in the town. New towns also hired sheriffs and deputies to keep peace in the streets. The hotheaded pistol wielders of the Wild West brought about some of the earliest arguments in favor of regulating Americans' right to carry guns wherever they went. As political scientist Robert J. Spitzer said, "Ironically, and contrary to legend, gun laws did more to settle the West than did guns."[6]

Guns on the Streets

The Wild West was not the only region of the United States where people tired of gun violence and demanded regulation. Big cities had their own problems with guns. In 1920, the U.S. government banned the production, sale, and transportation of all kinds of alcoholic beverages in the United States, which is known as Prohibition. Criminal gangs took over the illegal production, smuggling, and sale of alcoholic beverages to consumers. These gangs battled one another viciously, trying to gain an advantage over competitors and make more money in the alcohol trade. American cities, especially New York City and Chicago, Illinois, saw a higher level of gun violence than ever before in the nation.

Frightening new advancements in gun technology during Prohibition included the Thompson submachine gun, or Tommy gun. This rifle-style firearm could rapidly expel 20 to 30 bullets between reloading. In the hands of gang members, Tommy guns terrorized city streets. Mass murders and drive-by shootings—assassinations from within moving cars—became a public menace. "Competing organized crime groups engaged in spectacular assassinations and shootouts in public," wrote constitutional law professor James B. Jacobs. "The media and the public demanded a government response."[7]

The Tommy gun (shown here) was one of the first firearms to be subject to federal regulation.

In 1933, realizing Prohibition had sent crime spiraling out of control, the U.S. government repealed the ban on alcohol. It also made weapons such as the Tommy gun harder to find by passing the National Firearms Act in 1934 and the Federal Firearms Act in 1938. These laws required gun dealers to be licensed in order to sell weapons, put restrictions on the transfer of guns across state lines, and heavily taxed the possession of machine guns among private citizens. Thus, government control of alcohol ended at about the same time modern government control of firearms began.

Ironically, even though Prohibition brought public outcry for more regulation of guns, it also created a compelling argument that more regulation of the firearms industry might backfire. Just as people still bought and drank alcohol during Prohibition, opponents of gun control said people would still buy and use guns if they were outlawed. Many supporters of gun rights in America today argue that the lawlessness and gang power that was widespread during Prohibition would only be repeated if the government instituted a similar ban on guns. "Prohibition did not eliminate alcohol sales or consumption," wrote political science professor Harry L. Wilson. "Can we reasonably expect greater restrictions on firearms to reduce crime?"[8] Despite concern that gun control efforts might only echo the failure of Prohibition, the 1930s were not the last time American citizens would call for restrictions on firearm possession.

Firearms and the Fight for Civil Rights

A decade after Prohibition ended, the United States fought in World War II. A sense of national patriotism marked the era. Violent crime rates were low, and public calls for additional gun control faded. After the war was over, the United States became the site of a new kind of war: a public struggle for equal rights for its black citizens. The civil rights movement of the 1950s and 1960s was marked by considerable violence. Churches were bombed. Vehicles and buildings were set on fire. People assaulted one another and each other's property. Some of the most vivid, tragic attacks of the era were committed with guns.

Cities saw a tremendous increase in murders during the civil rights movement, and guns were the primary weapons being used. From 1964 to 1968, gun homicides increased 89 percent in the United States. In part as a reaction to the fear of being shot in their own neighborhoods, American citizens took part in a huge gun-buying spree. The nation's gun sales quadrupled, from 600,000 gun purchases in 1964 to 2.4 million in 1968. Firearms could be ordered through the mail in those days, making it impossible for law enforcement to keep track of who was buying guns.

Some of the earliest efforts at gun control were actually efforts to control certain groups by disarming them. Early in the nation's history, white people passed laws to prohibit free black people from

Martin Luther King Jr., a leader of the civil rights movement, was assassinated with a firearm on April 4, 1968.

A Brief History of the NRA

When most Americans think of the NRA, they think of a powerful pro-gun ownership organization that lobbies politicians and fights legal battles in an effort to preserve the Second Amendment. While this is what the NRA has evolved into, that was not always the case. The NRA was founded by a group of Union soldiers shortly after the American Civil War. They had noticed the sloppy gunmanship during the war and wanted to create an organization to sponsor shooting training and competitions. In fact, the NRA testified in favor of the first federal gun law in 1934, which aimed to reduce the number of machine guns on the streets. In the late 1950s, the NRA opened a new office with the stated goals of firearm safety education, marksmanship training, and shooting for recreation. In 1977, however, that all changed; the organization voted to move its headquarters from Virginia, near Washington, D.C., to Colorado. This showed that the organization was planning to be less involved in politics, which caused more than 1,000 NRA members to revolt. They voted out the leadership of the organization and replaced it with staunch Second Amendment supporters. Slowly, the NRA, which had always had a hand in politics as it voted against some of the stricter policies of gun control groups, became primarily political. It started advocating for mostly unrestricted individual gun ownership, and the original founders' ideals of safety, marksmanship, and a well-regulated militia fell by the wayside.

having guns. Even after the American Civil War, many states continued to enforce these laws. In the late 1800s, European immigrants arrived in the United States by the millions and were blamed for crime waves in cities. Local governments responded by requiring a permit to obtain a firearm and then refusing to grant permits to immigrants. During the civil rights movement, the white supremacist group known as the Ku Klux Klan (KKK) favored gun control measures that banned cheap handguns because poor Americans—especially black people, who have historically been disproportionately poorer than the rest of the population—often could not afford expensive firearms they could have used to defend themselves from attacks. Even today, taxing guns or ammunition, prohibiting sales of cheaper handguns, and charging high registration fees for firearms are seen as ways to make guns accessible only to certain classes and to prevent the poor from exercising their Second Amendment right.

A COMPLEX TOPIC

"Saying gun laws are always racist is just false … Saying that gun laws have never been racist is also just wrong."

–Saul Cornell, professor at Fordham University and gun control history researcher

Quoted in Creede Newton, "Gun Control's Racist Past and Present," *Al Jazeera*, October 6, 2017. www.aljazeera.com/indepth/features/2017/10/gun-control-racist-present-171006135904199.html

Americans widely blamed the lenient or nonexistent regulation of weapons in the 1960s for three of the most infamous crimes of the 20th century. The assassinations of President John F. Kennedy in November 1963, civil rights leader Martin Luther King Jr. in April 1968, and Senator Robert Kennedy in June 1968 increased the public outcry about how easy it was for people to get firearms—either legally or illegally. President Kennedy's assumed assassin, Lee Harvey Oswald, used a false name to place a mail order for the rifle he allegedly used in the murder. King's assassin, James Earl Ray, was a convicted armed robber and prison escapee who was legally banned from having firearms such as the rifle he used in the assassination. Senator Kennedy's killer, Palestinian immigrant Sirhan Sirhan, used a handgun in his crime, a weapon that American citizens increasingly disliked because its primary purpose was to shoot at other people rather than in sports such as hunting, the way rifles and shotguns were meant to be used.

Lee Harvey Oswald used a fake name to place a mail order for the gun he allegedly used to assassinate John F. Kennedy. He received the gun with no questions asked. Oswald himself was later assassinated with a handgun.

Renewed Call to (Dis)arms

The high-profile shootings of the 1960s became the basis for new gun legislation. According to historian Duncan Watts, "The Gun Control Act (1968) was passed following the assassinations of Martin Luther King Jr. and Robert Kennedy, when elected officials were again aware of a widespread public mood to curb gun ownership."[9] The act consisted of a group of federal laws that made gun purchase or possession illegal for people younger than 18, convicted felons (people who have committed a type of serious crime called a felony, which includes crimes such as murder, assault, burglary, and animal cruelty), anyone with a drug record, or anyone who has either been committed to a mental institution or has been, in the words of the law, "adjudicated as a mental defective." This means a judge has decided the person's actions, due to their mental illness, make them such a danger to themselves or others that some of their rights as citizens should be taken away. The new law also banned mail-order gun purchases and other methods of gun sales that crossed state borders, which made it easier to regulate who was buying and selling guns. Guns were given serial numbers to make individual weapons easier to track, and gun dealers, who now had to be federally licensed, were required to keep records of all gun sales and buyers.

RIGHTS AND RESPONSIBILITY

"Even a right must be exercised responsibly, and carrying a gun is a grave responsibility."

—Bruce N. Elmer, NRA certified law enforcement instructor

Bruce N. Elmer, *Armed: The Essential Guide to Concealed Carry.* Iola, WI: Gun Digest, 2012, p. 83.

The Gun Control Act of 1968 gave the federal government a better system for monitoring gun sales and possession in the United States, but it was unpopular with lawmakers and citizens who disliked the government's move to stretch its power over the states. "Gun rights supporters began almost immediately to press for legislation that would weaken or repeal the 1968 gun control laws, which they viewed as excessive and grossly unfair to law-abiding sportsmen,"[10] wrote political science professor Kristin A. Goss. To add to its growing unpopularity, the act also did not eliminate or even significantly reduce gun violence in the United States. Instead, the Federal Bureau of Investigation (FBI) reported that gun homicide rates increased steadily in the first five years after the new laws were passed. A decade after the Gun Control Act, gun violence in America was more widespread than ever. Firearms caused the deaths of almost as many people as car accidents did. The Gun Control Act had given the government more power to oversee firearms, their owners, and their sellers and buyers, but it had apparently done nothing to prevent gun violence.

Another Assassination Attempt

On March 30, 1981, the country witnessed another assassination attempt against a president. Ronald Reagan was waving to spectators on a sidewalk in Washington, D.C., when John Hinckley Jr., a member of the crowd, drew a revolver and fired six shots at him. One bullet entered Reagan's chest, puncturing his lung and narrowly missing his heart. Bullets also struck security officer Thomas Delahanty, Secret Service agent Tim McCarthy, and White House press secretary James Brady, who suffered a disabling head injury. Americans were alarmed that Hinckley, who stated that his actions had been intended to impress actress Jodie Foster and make her fall in love with him, had so easily obtained and used a handgun to try to kill the president. After the attack, Hinckley was evaluated by psychiatrists and diagnosed with schizotypal personality disorder, which includes symptoms such as detachment from reality and lack of emotion and empathy. However, since he had not been diagnosed previously, there was no record of his mental illness anywhere and therefore no reason for anyone to suspect he should not have been sold a gun—proving that the protections of the Gun Control Act of 1968 were not foolproof.

In the 1980s, Brady and his wife, Sarah, became involved in what would become known as the Brady Campaign to Prevent Handgun Violence and lobbied for the government to enact stricter gun control measures. In 1987, Congress considered a bill that would restrict gun purchases more than the 1968 act had done. It would require a waiting period between the time a gun was bought and the time the buyer could actually have it. During this period, police agencies would do a thorough background check on the buyer to see whether they were in any of the categories the 1968 act prohibited from owning a firearm. Under the Gun Control Act of 1968, formal background checks were not performed, and a customer could walk out of a store with a new weapon at the time of the purchase—something gun

After being shot in 1981, James Brady and his wife, Sarah, (both shown here) became outspoken advocates of gun control.

control supporters said was dangerous because the buyer might intend to go out and immediately shoot someone with the newly acquired weapon. Reagan himself supported the waiting period. "With the right to bear arms comes a great responsibility to use caution and common sense on handgun purchases," he said. "And it's just plain common sense that there be a waiting period to allow local law-enforcement officials to conduct background checks on those who wish to purchase handguns."[11]

Despite Reagan's support, some lawmakers still blocked the proposed legislation. For six years, Congress debated stricter government control over firearms. Finally, in November 1993, lawmakers approved the Brady Handgun Violence Prevention Act, named after James and Sarah Brady, and President Bill Clinton signed it into law. The Brady Act, which went into effect in early 1994, required a waiting period of five business days between the purchase of a gun and the day the customer could actually have it. During this period, police had to confirm that the buyer was a legal U.S. citizen with no felony convictions, no known current drug addiction, no history of domestic violence, and no dishonorable discharge from the military, and who had not been committed to a mental institution or adjudicated as a mental defective. The waiting period requirement of the Brady Act expired five years later, partially because a national instant background check program could generally confirm in only a few moments whether a buyer was legally cleared to own a gun. This means background checks can be completed before the buyer even leaves the shop. However, some states have set their own waiting period requirements. One of the main reasons for imposing a waiting period is to prevent people from impulsively committing a violent act. For instance, someone who has made up their mind to commit suicide in a state with no waiting period could go out, buy a gun, and kill themselves immediately. With a waiting period in place, they would have to wait several days and might change their mind about killing themselves.

Although some gun rights supporters oppose waiting periods on the basis that they believe any gun control measure abuses their rights, gun control advocates believe that for people such as hunters or recreational shooters who do not want a gun for any criminal purpose, minor controls such as waiting periods and background checks are not an infringement on lifestyle or rights.

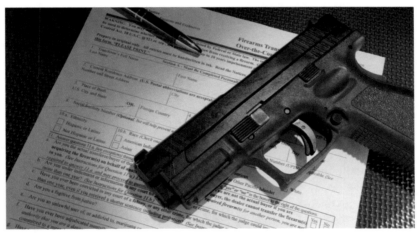

Background checks are a hotly debated aspect of gun control. Some people believe submitting to a background check infringes on law-abiding citizens' rights, while others see it as an essential part of controlling gun violence.

Gun Control Does Not Control Criminals

Gun control advocates viewed the passage of the Brady Act as a major victory in the fight against gun violence. Although 1993 was a peak year for murder in the United States, by 1998, five years after the Brady Act was passed, the FBI reported that murder rates had dropped to their lowest point since 1967. However, researchers found that waiting periods and background checks for gun purchases had little or nothing to do with the declining murder rate. Before the Brady Act, 18 states had already required waiting periods and background checks for gun purchases. After the Brady Act, the remaining 32 states were forced to follow the new rules as well. Gun crime rates fell at the same rate in both groups of states, suggesting that something besides the new, stricter law was causing the drop in crime rates. Furthermore, all violent crime in the United States declined at the same rate during this period, not just gun-related crime. Americans, it seemed, were more peaceful in general, which made it hard to determine whether stricter gun control had an impact on shootings at all.

In 1994, the Brady Campaign to Prevent Handgun Violence claimed background checks had kept guns out of the hands of 40,000 buyers, a statistic widely used to prove the success of the law. However, the act did nothing to address guns sold from dealers who had no license, which law enforcement experts pointed out was the way most criminals had always obtained their guns. People who could not pass the background check still got their hands on weapons; they just did it illegally from dealers who did not comply with background checks. "In retrospect we would not expect Brady to be effective against violent crime," said Philip Cook, a Duke University researcher who studied the consequences of the Brady Act. "Increasingly homicides are committed by career criminals who do not get their guns in legal ways."[12]

Another gun control measure was also controversially called a success in the years after it passed. In 1994, Clinton signed a ban on assault weapons—firearms designed specifically to harm or kill other people. Crime rates fell, but they had been on the decline throughout the 1990s, even before the Federal Assault Weapons Ban. The ban was scheduled to sunset, or expire, after 10 years. As the 2004 sunset date approached, many Americans worried that once the ban on assault weapons was lifted, the falling crime rate would be reversed and the country would see a dramatic rise in gun-related violence committed by assault weapons. However, once assault weapons were again legalized, crime rates only continued to drop, implying that the ban had had little effect on gun crime after all.

In 2011, seven years after the assault weapons ban was lifted, the national murder rate had dropped to half of what it

America's First Gun Control Agency

In the 1790s, shortly after the American Revolution, the government first imposed taxes on alcohol and tobacco and created a department to regulate those substances, which also included agents who caught people who were not paying their taxes. During Prohibition, the department had even greater responsibilities, such as catching alcohol smugglers. In the 1930s, the country's problems with gangsters and guns prompted the government to add firearms to the department's responsibilities. It became known as the Bureau of Alcohol, Tobacco, and Firearms, or ATF. In the 1970s, the government added explosives to things the ATF oversees, making its official name the Bureau of Alcohol, Tobacco, Firearms and Explosives, although it is still abbreviated to ATF. Today, the ATF supports law enforcement agencies all over the country, helping with investigations into arson (deliberately burning down buildings), matching guns to the bullets fired from them, creating gang resistance education programs, and helping investigate some of the most violent crimes in the nation. In 2003, the ATF became part of the U.S. Department of Justice. It is the government's official agency responsible for enforcing firearm laws in America.

was in 1991 and the lowest point in almost 50 years. Crime researchers have concluded that there is much more to violent crime in the United States than the mere presence or absence of guns. Nevertheless, supporters of both sides of the gun control argument continue to make strong cases in favor of their own position to allow or restrict weapons in the hands of Americans, keeping the debate over gun control active today.

CHAPTER 2

Guns and the Law

All three branches of the U.S. government have had a role in gun control throughout history. The legislative branch—Congress, which is made up of the House of Representatives and the Senate—has the power to make new laws such as the Gun Control Act of 1968 or the Brady Act of 1994. It also has the power to vote either to extend certain laws, such as the 10-year Assault Weapons Ban of 1994, or let them expire. The executive branch, which consists of the president and their advisors, either signs the legislative branch's ideas into national law, as Bill Clinton did with the Brady Act, or denies legislation with a veto. The judicial branch, which consists of the federal court system headed by the Supreme Court, makes judgments about whether laws are allowed by the U.S. Constitution. Controversy over gun control affects government at all levels.

This system of checks and balances is one of the reasons why it is so difficult to enact meaningful gun reform. In 2018, Ohio governor John Kasich, a Republican, assembled a bipartisan panel—one that included both Republicans and Democrats—to discuss possible options for gun reform in his state. Everyone at the panel was in favor of the Second Amendment but also wanted to keep people safer. They produced a legislative bill package that was introduced to the Republican-controlled legislature by a Republican lawmaker. Kasich was disappointed that even though the bill was bipartisan and upheld the ideals of the Second Amendment, the bill failed to pass.

The Right to Bear Arms

The meaning of the Second Amendment has long been the source of legal challenges. It was created with the goal of stopping government efforts to prohibit citizens from purchasing or owning firearms. People on both sides of the debate have questioned everything from the amendment's grammar and word choice to what the authors of the Bill of Rights meant when they wrote it in the late 1700s.

Many who oppose gun control say the Second Amendment clearly defines ownership of guns as a right of every American when it says "the right of the people to keep and bear arms shall not be infringed." Not only does the amendment guarantee citizens the right to have guns, they say, it states that this right shall not be violated. "Man has natural, unalienable rights. Among these are the rights to life, liberty, and property," wrote historian Benedict D. LaRosa in 2001. "If he possesses these rights, then he must also possess a right to defend them. If he has a right to defend them, then he has a right to the means with which to defend them … The Founders were so adamant about protecting

Many people have a strong attachment to the Second Amendment. Shown here is Lauren Boebert, owner of the Second Amendment-themed Shooters Grill in Rifle, Colorado. The café's staff and patrons are encouraged to openly carry their guns in the establishment.

the right of every individual to keep and bear arms, they pro-hibited even trespassing upon the fringes or outer edges of that right."[13] Those who read the Second Amendment this way tend to view gun control measures of any kind as unconstitutional.

While the second half of the amendment is often read liter-ally by gun rights supporters, the first half is what gun control activists frequently focus on. They read the phrase "a well-regulated militia being necessary to the security of a free state" to mean that the right of the people to keep and bear arms is only for the purpose of establishing a trained military force. "Leading up to the adoption of the Constitution and the Bill of Rights, no law in any of the states, colonies, or territories had used the phrase 'bear arms' in anything but a military sense," said Second Amendment researcher Patrick J. Charles. "The use of the phrase 'bear arms' was distinctively limited to use in each of the colonies' militia laws."[14] A militia in the late 1700s was an army made up of citizens rather than a professional army of paid soldiers. In 1791, Americans believed very strongly in a militia, which had helped them win independence from Britain, but in the 21st century, a militia is no longer the main way the United States protects itself. If the Second Amendment means citizens can only be armed as part of a regulated militia, this could outdate the entire amendment.

The idea that the Second Amendment could be repealed is frightening to many gun rights advocates. After the Parkland shooting, for example, the NRA's executive vice president, Wayne LaPierre, wrote that gun control advocates want "to eliminate the Second Amendment and our firearms freedoms so they can eradicate all individual freedoms."[15] However, this highly charged statement has no evidence to support it. While some people think the amendment should be repealed, most gun control advocates do not want to ban all guns; their main goal is to make it harder for dangerous people to get guns legally.

Relevant Court Cases

The Supreme Court made its first decision about the Second Amendment in 1876 when it ruled that the Constitution did not grant the right to keep and bear arms—but it said the

COMMON SENSE RESTRICTIONS

"All we really want are sensible restrictions based on public safety and common sense ... Go ahead, buy a gun. Use it to hunt, for target practice, in a collection, or in case you need to defend your home. Just register it and submit to a background check."

—Andrew Rosenthal, *New York Times* columnist

Andrew Rosenthal, "The Gun Lobby and Military Suicides," *New York Times*, November 8, 2011. taking-note.blogs.nytimes.com/2011/11/08/the-gun-lobby-and-military-suicides.

Constitution did not grant the First Amendment rights to free speech and religion, either. These were fundamental human rights people already had before the Constitution was ever written, the ruling stated, and the federal government did not have the power to give people these freedoms or to take them away. The court thus upheld the idea that Americans could rightly possess and use firearms the same way they could speak freely and practice their chosen religion.

In 1939, the Supreme Court heard another case about the right to keep and bear arms. This case was about whether the Second Amendment applied to any kind of gun a citizen might want to possess. Through the National Firearms Act of 1934, which the NRA supported, Congress put limits on the right to own certain kinds of weapons—in particular, machine gun–style weapons popular among the brutal street gangs of the 1920s and 1930s. Shortly after the National Firearms Act was passed, a man named Jack Miller was charged with owning a newly regulated assault weapon. Miller argued that the National Firearms Act violated the Second Amendment. In *United States v. Miller*, the Supreme Court decided that Miller or any other American citizen could own one of the banned weapons only if they could prove the weapon was specifically for use in a regulated militia, as the Second Amendment mentioned. The 1939 ruling did not state that citizens could never own a restricted or banned weapon, but that they would have to justify their purpose for owning one.

The court's decision was taken to mean that the Second Amendment supported the idea of a militia more than a particular citizen's right to own weapons—which was a highly controversial view. "The *Miller* decision was widely accepted by the federal courts of appeals as evidencing a *rejection* of an individual right to keep and bear arms," said former Supreme Court law clerk Earl E. Pollack. "This consensus was sharply challenged by what became a flood of scholarly articles based on new analysis of the history and purpose of the Second Amendment."[16]

The arguments about the right to keep and bear arms continued into the 21st century. In 2008, another landmark case about the Second Amendment landed in the Supreme Court. The city of Washington, D.C., had prohibited any of its citizens from owning or carrying a handgun since 1976. In 2008, the Supreme Court heard a case, known as *District of Columbia v. Heller*, involving Dick Heller, a security guard for the city. Heller carried a handgun every day for his job but was forced to leave it at work at the end of every shift. City law forbade him to keep a handgun in his own home for self-protection. He sued the city, saying the Second Amendment gave him the right to keep a handgun at home.

JUDGES RULE ON A CASE-BY-CASE BASIS

"In concluding that Americans have the right to keep guns in the home for self-defense, the court was careful not to categorically reject all regulation … they are not convinced that … regulations violate the fundamental liberty enshrined in the amendment—any more than a noise restriction in a residential neighborhood or a ban on highway billboards violates the First Amendment."

–Steve Chapman, reporter

Steve Chapman, "Column: Why the Second Amendment Is Irrelevant," *Chicago Tribune*, February 23, 2018. www.chicagotribune.com/news/opinion/chapman/ct-perspec-chapman-second-amendment-20180223-story.html.

The Supreme Court ruled in Heller's favor, stating that the Second Amendment does indeed give citizens the right to keep and bear arms, including handguns. Because of this, the court ruled that the city's practice of banning all handguns was unconstitutional. The *District of Columbia v. Heller* decision was seen as a major step in favor of Second Amendment rights and gun ownership for Americans.

From 1976 to 2008, citizens in Washington, D.C., were not allowed to own a handgun—a firearm that can be held, carried, and fired using only one hand, such as a pistol or revolver.

Rights and Regulations

In the *District of Columbia v. Heller* case, the Supreme Court interpreted the Second Amendment as guaranteeing people the right to own firearms, including handguns. However, this does not mean the court guarantees all citizens the right to own any weapon they choose. Assault weapons, which are generally defined as firearms that can shoot in a semiautomatic or fully automatic mode, have been a continuing subject of the gun control debate. A semiautomatic weapon fires a single bullet with each pull of the trigger and automatically reloads a bullet into the

The Gun Show Loophole

One of the major issues being debated in the wake of the Parkland shooting is known as the "gun show loophole." People who use this term are generally advocating for gun control and using the phrase to refer to a situation where people buy a gun from someone at a gun show and are not subject to a background check the way they would be if they bought the weapon at a regular store. Some gun rights advocates have stated that this loophole does not actually exist because no particular law singles out gun shows. Research by the nonpartisan (not favoring one political party) website PolitiFact brought some clarity to the issue with three main points:

- *Federally licensed gun sellers are required to run background checks. But not all sellers are required to be licensed. Some of those unlicensed sellers sell at gun shows ... private sellers without a federal license don't have to meet the same requirement. Though this exception is often referred to as the "gun show loophole," it actually applies more broadly to unlicensed individuals, whether they are selling at a gun show or somewhere else.*

- *It's not clear how many sellers are licensed and how many are not. Some studies are out of date ... Professors at Northeastern and Harvard universities conducted a gun survey in 2015 ... The national survey of 4,000 non-institutionalized adults found that 22 percent of the people who purchased guns—at gun shows, stores or elsewhere—underwent no background check ... When researchers excluded purchases between family and friends, that number dropped to 15 percent, which equates to approximately 5 million gun owners whose most recent purchase did not involve a background check.*

- *Experts warn that the phrase "gun show loophole" is imprecise at best. But people do buy guns without having to undergo background checks ... UCLA law professor Adam Winkler said[,] "What is called the gun-show loophole is misnamed. It should be the 'private sale loophole' or the 'background check loophole' ... The reason people talk about gun shows is that they are easily accessible marketplaces for people who don't want to be subject to a background check to find non-licensed gun sellers." Gabriel Chin, a professor at UC Davis School of Law, told PolitiFact that there is a loophole in the sense that it has not been clear how many firearms one has to sell before one is required to obtain a license.*[1]

1. Amy Sherman, "PolitiFact Sheet: 3 Things to Know About the 'Gun Show Loophole,'" PolitiFact, January 7, 2016. www.politifact.com/truth-o-meter/article/2016/jan/07/politifact-sheet-3-things-know-about-gun-show-loop/

chamber from the ammunition compartment (the clip) until all the bullets have been shot. An automatic weapon works similarly but instead sprays bullets until the shooter releases the trigger. Gun control laws have banned such assault weapons over the years. In 1994, Congress also banned any gun with certain features that gave it an assault purpose, such as a folding stock (the handle or shoulder piece to which the barrel of the gun attaches), a pistol grip that allows users to hold a rifle like a handgun, or a flash suppressor (a device that attaches to the end of a gun barrel to hide the sudden burst of flame emitted when the gun is fired).

People who use guns for legal reasons such as hunting or self-defense are unlikely to need either a flash suppressor or a fully automatic weapon. "What ... use is there for one of these assault weapons?" asked former Pennsylvania governor Ed Rendell, a supporter of the bans. "What American needs an assault weapon to protect themselves?"[17]

On the other hand, bans on assault-style weapons may unfairly assume their owners plan to use them for crime. Not until a person has committed a crime can they be considered a criminal, and simply owning a particular weapon does not mean a person will use it against others. Many gun rights defenders therefore interpret these gun control efforts as a limit on their constitutional freedoms. "'Who needs an assault weapon?' is an illegitimate question," claimed the NRA. "In a free society, the burden of proof is not upon those who wish to exercise rights, it is upon those who wish to restrict rights."[18] Furthermore, guns that are classified as military-style assault weapons make up a very small percentage of all weapons used in actual crimes. According to LaPierre, the bigger problem to focus on is the practice of straw purchasing, which is a term for when people with clean backgrounds buy weapons for criminals who want to get around a background check. This is similar to someone who is 21 or older buying alcohol to give to younger friends or relatives. The practice of banning assault weapons, therefore, has little effect on curbing crimes committed with guns. Some gun control advocates acknowledge this but argue that the laws would still be worthwhile because they would limit the number of people who could be killed or injured at one time in a shooting spree.

Taking Aim at Handguns

The type of guns used in the vast majority of gun-related crimes in the United States are not assault-style weapons at all but handguns. A handgun's small size makes it easy to carry, hide under clothing, or store in a home or vehicle. In part because they are so portable, handguns are by far the most common type of firearm used by criminals in America. According to a report by the FBI, about 73 percent of murders in the United States were committed with firearms in 2016, and handguns are used in murders two to three times as often as any other kind of gun.

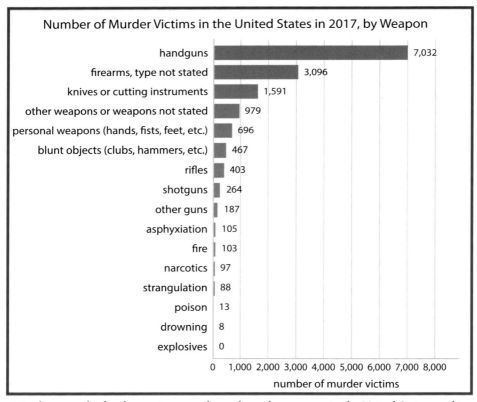

Handguns are by far the most commonly used murder weapons in the United States, as this information from the FBI shows.

Regulating handguns more strictly, therefore, would arguably have a far larger effect on crime than regulating assault weapons.

Gun rights activists, however, use the same argument against banning handguns as they do against banning assault weapons— just because someone owns a handgun does not mean they are going to use it to commit a crime. "Anti-gun people persist in believing that their neighbors and co-workers will become mass murderers if allowed to own firearms," said psychiatrist and gun rights activist Sarah Thompson, but "the anti-gun person who believes that malicious shootings by ordinary gun owners are likely to occur is not in touch with reality."[19] Handguns appeal to noncriminals for many of the same reasons they appeal to criminals—they are smaller, more lightweight, easier to store, and easier to load and fire than long guns such as rifles and shotguns. This makes them well suited for self-defense. Criminals may use handguns more than any other type of weapon, but banning the weapons would prevent law-abiding citizens from owning this popular type of gun as well.

Open Carry versus Concealed Carry

Much of the gun control issue has centered on regulating what types of guns are or should be available to citizens, such as handguns or assault weapons. Other efforts to control gun violence have to do with where and how people are allowed to use and store their firearms. A gun kept at home is unlikely to be used for crime, but guns carried outside of one's home are far more likely to be fired, with potentially deadly consequences. Whether people should have a right to carry a firearm with them when they leave their home—specifically, a portable handgun that is easy to conceal—is another debated aspect of gun control.

U.S. citizens, lawmakers, and government officials have debated concealed carry policies for about two centuries. During the 1800s, the Wild West provided examples of the dangers of armed citizens in the streets. Criminals carried handguns, and therefore, many law-abiding citizens felt they were safer if they did too. If someone drew a weapon, several bystanders were likely to pull out their own guns. Such tense situations sometimes led to shootouts, and any innocent bystander could be caught in the crossfire. Citizens of the Wild West quickly took steps to stop lawless gun shooting. "Even in the most violence-prone western towns, gunplay and lawlessness were only briefly tolerated,"[20] wrote political science professor Robert J. Spitzer.

DANGER ON THE HOME FRONT

"The risk does not come from homicidal maniacs or muggers or rapists. The risk comes from people using their own guns to shoot themselves or their family members."

—Shankar Vedantam, social science correspondent for NPR

Shankar Vedantam, *The Hidden Brain: How Our Unconscious Minds Elect Presidents, Control Markets, Wage Wars, and Save Our Lives*. New York, NY: Spiegel & Grau, 2010, p. 235.

The debate around whether people should conceal (hide) their weapons or carry them openly (visibly) has been raging for decades. In fact, the most recent wave of gun control restrictions started in 1967 with a California state law that was signed to prevent open carry. That year, in the midst of the civil rights movement, a militant black rights group called the Black Panthers protested the mistreatment of black Americans—particularly the violence they faced—by standing "on the steps of the California statehouse armed with .357 Magnums, 12-gauge shotguns and .45-caliber pistols and announced, 'The time has come for black people to arm themselves.'"[21] This incident frightened white people so much that Ronald Reagan, who was the governor of California at the time, passed the Mulford Act, which banned the open carrying of loaded guns. The NRA originally supported this law because many of its members were white and felt threatened by the Black Panthers, but as more gun control laws began to be passed, the organization switched its stance and started advocating more for open carry laws.

There are many arguments surrounding the open carry versus concealed carry debate, and each side tends to believe their preferred policy is the safest one. Open carry advocates

Concealed carry laws were passed in California after members of the Black Panther Party legally carried guns openly and called for other black Americans to arm themselves.

generally say that seeing a gun can deter someone who might otherwise try to commit a crime. They also say that it can prevent arguments from escalating into deadly shootings—if someone is already aware that a person is armed, they can act accordingly, rather than being surprised when someone pulls out a gun. Advocates of concealed carry, on the other hand, say open carry can have the opposite effect: Seeing someone with a gun can make others nervous and cause ordinary arguments to escalate when two people with guns feel threatened by each other. Many gun control activists favor laws that do not forbid people to own guns but do forbid them to carry a gun in public places, either openly or concealed. While gun rights activists tend to support a person's right to carry a weapon in public, most believe individuals should make the choice not do so if they have not been trained on how to safely carry and use the weapon.

As of early 2019, five states—California, Florida, Illinois, New York, and South Carolina—as well as the District of Columbia ban open carry. All other states have laws allowing at least some citizens to carry loaded weapons, although most states require a person to have a special license or permit in order to carry a gun in public, and this permit dictates whether the gun must be visible or can be concealed. To receive such a permit, a person typically must pass classes to prove they are knowledge-able about gun safety and know how to use a gun properly. Most states' permits also require a criminal background check of the applicant, and the permit generally only applies in the state in which it was issued. States that allow open carry often limit the places people can go with a visible weapon, in part because the sight of a gun can be intimidating to fellow citizens or could confuse police officers should a crime occur. States that offer concealed carry permits often restrict the places where a citizen can have a gun as well. For example, weapons may be forbidden in state or federal buildings and on school campuses.

Whether law-abiding U.S. citizens should be allowed to carry loaded firearms, either concealed or visible, is an ongoing part of the gun controversy. Even with restrictions on carried weapons, gun control activists say public places are more dan-gerous if people can walk around armed. On the other hand, say gun rights activists, criminals pay no attention to laws and will not hesitate to carry hidden guns and pull them out to use them in public places, so law-abiding citizens should be able to carry a loaded gun of their own for self-defense if they choose. "The problem with concealed weapons is that criminals carry them and use them against their victims," wrote economist Fred E. Foldvary in 1999 in an opinion piece for *Progress Report*. "But criminals are already outside the law, so they carry the weapon law or no law. Concealed weapon permit holders are seldom the perpetrators of violent crimes."[22]

The issue of permits to carry guns is one of the most hotly de-bated aspects of gun control. States pass their own laws to allow or deny citizens the right to carry any loaded firearm in public, either openly or concealed. Each state can choose between "may issue" and "shall issue" policies. "May issue" means permits are given out on a case-by-case basis after the government studies the person's application. "Shall issue" means the state grants a permit to any applicant who meets basic requirements such as minimum age. Each state has different policies regarding open carry permits and concealed carry permits, and some are not

Printing Weapons

One of the newest challenges for gun control advocates is that it is now possible to legally get a gun without purchasing one. In 2013, Cody Wilson uploaded plans for what he called the Liberator, a gun that that can be made at home with a 3-D printer. The gun is made almost completely from plastic, aside from a metal firing pin (Wilson's design uses a screw) and a piece of steel included solely to make the weapon visible to metal detectors, but it is capable of firing standard handgun rounds. These guns can go completely undetected if all the metal is removed from them, and without any serial numbers or way to trace who is printing them, they are effectively invisible to law enforcement. These innovations make it even harder for guns to be regulated and for police to track down who commits crimes with them. They are easier to destroy than metal guns, so a murder weapon could be easily disposed of after a crime. In addition, since 3-D printers are accessible to anyone who can afford one, acquiring a gun without going through a background check would be easier than ever. The laws concerning these "ghost guns" are still being debated and refined as of 2019, but in September 2018, 19 states filed a lawsuit to block Wilson from distributing his gun design online.

Shown here is Cody Wilson with the Liberator, the 3-D-printed gun he designed.

The Debate Over Bump Stocks

A bump-fire stock, also known as a bump stock, is an accessory that can be attached to a semiautomatic rifle to make it shoot nearly as fast as an automatic weapon. Bump stocks first became a topic of debate in 2017 when a shooter opened fire on concert attendees in Las Vegas, Nevada. His use of this accessory enabled him to kill nearly 60 people and injure about 400 more in a matter of minutes, which led to calls for it to be banned. The debate died down eventually but resurfaced again after the Parkland shooting. Nikolas Cruz did not use a bump stock, but his actions made people think of how much higher the death toll could have been if he had.

The main arguments some gun rights advocates use for keeping bump stocks legal have generally been that they are fun to use at a shooting range and that restricting one aspect of gun ownership may eventually lead to the government banning guns completely. Mel Bernstein, owner of a gun store in Colorado, voiced the thoughts of many gun rights supporters when he said, "If you're a law-abiding citizen in America and you have a clean record, you should be able to own anything you want."[1] However, the fact that they are so deadly led politicians, former soldiers, thousands of gun owners, and even the NRA to support bump stock regulation. As California senator Dianne Feinstein noted, "The only reason to modify a gun is to kill as many people as possible in as short a time as possible."[2] This opposition to bump stocks paid off in November 2018 when the administration of President Donald Trump outlawed them. However, only one month later, the organization Gun Owners of America stated that it would file a lawsuit against the ATF to try to get the decision reversed, showing that sometimes not even a change in a law puts a debate to rest.

Shown here is a semiautomatic rifle equipped at the back with a bump stock. To the right is the magazine, which holds the bullets.

1. Quoted in Chris Welch, "Could Ban on Bump Stocks Bring Real Change to Gun Control?," WXYZ Detroit, November 29, 2018. www.wxyz.com/news/national/could-ban-on-bump-stock-bring-real-change-to-gun-control.
2. Quoted in Grace Donnelly, "What You Need to Know About Bump Stock Gun Accessories," Fortune, February 21, 2018. fortune.com/2018/02/21/bump-stocks-ban-las-vegas-shooting/.

valid in other states. Therefore, people who are interested in carrying a gun should make sure they are in compliance with the local laws at all times.

Guns or Ammunition?

In addition to permits, controlling ammunition by limiting the type and quantity of bullets a person can buy or own has long been seen as a way to lessen the potential danger of guns. A typical person who owns a handgun for self-defense should not antici- pate needing hundreds of bullets on hand to fight off an attacker, whereas someone with criminal intentions may stock up on these bullets before going on a shooting spree. Because of this, restrict- ing ammunition—or even outlawing certain kinds—is another approach to gun control.

Because bullets themselves do not require background checks and are widely available, it is difficult to keep track of how many bullets one person buys or possesses. In 2018, the Gun Violence Prevention and Safe Communities Act was introduced in Congress. The act would increase federal taxes on both guns and ammunition as a way to curb problems with gun violence. If bullets were more expensive, people would be less likely to buy many at once. They would instead be likely to buy and keep only the minimal ammunition they needed for self-protection or hunting. If the bill was passed, the tax money would go toward funding things such as community-based policing—a method of law enforcement where the police get to know the people in a neighborhood, making them less likely to arrest someone based on how they look or act at a particular moment—projects to reduce gun violence, and research into gun violence trends by the Centers for Disease Control and Prevention (CDC).

A gun with no bullets, gun rights activists reason, is as use- less as having no gun at all, so ammunition regulation is really a form of gun control. Even raising the price of ammunition through reduced availability or taxes is seen as unfair to many people in America. Many gun supporters see such regulations and taxes on bullets as a sneaky way for gun control activists to get around the Second Amendment, preventing or discouraging people from exercising their constitutional rights. Others have noted that a tax would hurt law-abiding citizens who routinely shoot for sport rather than the criminals the law is aimed at; for instance, a mass shooter would only need to buy one or two boxes of ammunition to commit their crime, while a hunter buys far more than that every year.

Economists have pointed out other problems with the proposed 2018 tax bill. In an article for *TaxVox*, a blog run by the Tax Policy Center, tax researcher Robert McClelland pointed out, "A recent RAND study found that hunters are not responsive to price changes in the form of higher license fees. If all gun purchasers are like those hunters, raising taxes will have little or no effect on gun sales."[23] Instead, he believes, more people may start buying their guns at gun shows, where the tax would not apply. This would have the added effect of reducing the number of background checks that are done, which means the tax bill might have no positive effect at all, only a negative one. This is another example of how there is no single perfect solution to the problem of gun violence; when creating gun control policies, multiple angles must be considered at the same time.

Ready, Aim, Debate

As arguments over ammunition affordability show, proposed regulations on firearms are not just about guns but are linked to beliefs about social classes, the causes and consequences of crime, and the very meaning of the Constitution. There are no easy answers in the gun control debate, but because gun ownership is seen as a life-and-death topic, it is one of the most emotionally charged issues in the United States today. Ongoing arguments for and against it create complex dilemmas. Meanwhile, activists on both sides tend to misrepresent facts or skew statistics to suit their own arguments. Fully understanding the issue involves a careful consideration of the concerns and opinions of those who favor stricter gun control and those who oppose it, and they both argue passionately for their views.

The Gun Control Side

G uns result in the death of 35,000 people on average every year in the United States via murder, suicide, and accidents. Another 70,000 people per year are wounded by gunfire. In fact, more Americans have died from gun wounds since 1968 than in all U.S. wars combined. Homicide is most frequently in the news, and the high rate of gun homicides tends to be seen as a uniquely American problem. In 2014, the *Onion*, a satirical publication, published an article titled, "'No Way to Prevent This,' Says Only Nation Where This Regularly Happens," which was a sarcastic way of pointing

Gun control advocates believe changes need to be made to keep people safe.

out that the mass shootings the United States experiences fairly regularly are not as common in most other countries. Gun control advocates frequently share the fictional article on social media, and the *Onion* reposts it after every mass shooting to make the point that something in the United States needs to change.

A 2018 study published in the *Journal of the American Medical Association (JAMA)* found that the United States is one of only six countries in the world that make up half of all gun deaths. The United States, which is responsible for 14.8 percent of the worldwide total, is surpassed only by Brazil. While it makes sense that two of the largest countries in the world have the highest number of gun deaths, the United States is unique among these six countries—which also include Mexico, Colombia, Venezuela, and Guatemala—because it is one of the wealthiest. The website Vox explained,

> *For comparison, the US's rate of 10.6 gun deaths per 100,000 people was much higher than Switzerland's rate of 2.8, Canada's 2.1, Germany's 0.9, the United Kingdom's 0.3, and Japan's 0.2.*
>
> *It is expected that as countries become wealthier and build stronger government institutions, they will see fewer gun deaths (since systemic poverty and weak criminal justice systems, for example, can contribute to more violence). While the rate of US gun deaths is lower than that of many less developed countries, America is still an outlier when compared to nations in similar socioeconomic circumstances.*[24]

While it is possible that some countries have underreported their own rates of gun violence, this is the most comprehensive study so far.

In addition to having a large population, Americans own about 40 percent of the world's guns. Statistically, the United States sees the most gun violence of any country in the world and also has the highest rate of gun ownership per person. These statistics support arguments that the United States would be safer if its government regulated guns more strictly.

A SATIRICAL CRITICISM

"[R]esidents of the only economically advanced nation in the world where roughly two mass shootings have occurred every month for the past five years were referring to themselves and their situation as 'helpless.'"

—the *Onion*

"'No Way to Prevent This,' Says Only Nation Where This Regularly Happens," *Onion*, May 27, 2014. www.theonion.com/no-way-to-prevent-this-says-only-nation-where-this-r-1819576527.

Murder by Gun

Murder is the fear people tend to associate most with guns. Homicides are much more common in the United States than in other nations with a comparable standard of living, such as Canada, Japan, and the countries of Europe. In 2016, approximately 5 Americans per 100,000 were intentionally murdered, according to the United Nations International Homicide Statistics—far higher than the reported rates of an average 1.4 per 100,000 in the UK and Canada and 0.3 per 100,000 in Japan. Also in 2016, the latest available statistics from the CDC concluded that more than 14,000 people were murdered with guns.

Gun rights advocates frequently say things such as, "Guns don't kill people, people kill people," or "It's not the gun that's the problem, it's the person behind the gun." While it is true that firearms by themselves do not hurt anyone, guns are very effective tools for someone who wants to injure or kill others. In 2018, the *Washington Post* analyzed federal homicide statistics that the CDC had kept since 1910. According to the data, there was a spike in gun homicides between 2014 and 2016. While the overall homicide rate rose by less than 2 percent in that time period, the gun homicide rate rose by more than 30 percent, from 11,000 to well over 14,000. In 2016, gun homicides accounted for 74.5 percent of all homicides in the United States, which is the highest share in more than 80 years.

Should Cars Be Banned Too?

The issue of gun control is heated and often leads people to make extreme statements. Gun rights advocates who believe gun control advocates want to ban all guns sometimes draw a comparison to car crashes. As a way to show that the other side's argument is silly, they ask whether cars should be banned as well, since they can be used to kill people. In addition to unintentional crashes, some people have used cars to deliberately run into other people when they had no other weapon handy.

In an article for the *Huffington Post*, lawyer Gavin Magrath responded to the comparison between guns and cars. He wrote,

> *No one is suggesting we ban all cars—and no one is suggesting we ban all guns … It's not even on the table. It's a red herring designed to prevent reasonable debate and discussion …*

> *But* cars kill people, or more accurately, people driving cars kill people, *just as* people shooting guns kill people … *No one would ban cars (or guns) but we do (and should) require:*

> • *licensing with written and practical tests;*
>
> • *frequent renewal including updated photo and medical questionnaire;*
>
> • *specialty licensing and training for specialty products;*
>
> • *product registration and mandatory liability insurance policy;*
>
> • *effective enforcement of product safety and use regulations;*
>
> • *key locks and other anti-theft devices;*
>
> • *manufacturer-funded safety research;*
>
> • *adoption by manufacturers of identified best safety features in spite of additional cost;*
>
> • *industry or publicly funded awareness and safety campaigns; and*
>
> • *restriction of high-performance, unsafe products to private courses/ranges.*

> *We already do every single one of those things with motor vehicles. When we finally woke up to the problem of drunk driving we tightened DUI regulation and enforcement and no one ever complained that we wanted to ban cars.*[1]

1. Gavin Magrath, "For 2013, Let's Ban Cars and Guns," *Huffington Post*, last updated March 5, 2013. www.huffingtonpost.com/gavin-magrath/gun-control-debate_b_2389047.html.

Even if someone is not killed by a gun, gunshot injuries can be devastating. Twice the number of people killed by guns live through being shot, and a bullet wound may affect them for life. Gunshot wounds can permanently impair a victim, especially if the brain or spinal cord is injured. A victim may live through a shooting but have lifelong disabilities.

While mass shootings are frequently in the news and have captured the public's fears, a far more common—and far less frequently discussed—issue with guns is their use in domestic violence situations. Studies have shown that when a gun is kept in the house, women in abusive relationships are about five times more likely to be killed by their partners than women whose partners do not keep a gun in the house. Additionally, according to the Giffords Law Center to Prevent Gun Violence, "domestic violence assaults involving a gun are 12 times more likely to end in death than assaults with other weapons or physical harm ... In 2011, nearly two-thirds of women killed with guns were killed by their intimate partners."[25]

Research has shown that having a gun in the house greatly increases the likelihood that a domestic violence situation will end in tragedy.

Domestic violence is not unrelated to mass shootings. Experts say domestic abuse is often an indicator that a person will shoot someone besides their original victim. National Public Radio (NPR) reported that more than 50 percent of recent American mass shootings were committed by someone who was abusive to their partner or family members. In fact, Nikolas Cruz was reported by classmates to have been abusive to his ex-girlfriend and to have fought with her new boyfriend. His violent behavior caused at least three students to report him to school officials before the date of the Parkland shooting. Additionally, several neighbors and even Cruz's own mother reported his violent or illegal behavior to police officers in the years before he carried out his attack.

The pattern of domestic abuse and gun violence has become so undeniable that it has led some states to change their laws. In 2018, Oregon passed a law to close the "boyfriend loophole" in its gun control policy. The new law "would allow police in Oregon to confiscate guns from people who stalk or abuse a partner even if they are not married to or living with the victim and do not share a child in common with the victim."[26] As of 2019, 22 other states have similar laws. Reporting this type of harassment and other forms of abuse can potentially help police keep an eye on someone who might become violent.

However, as the situation with Cruz shows, reporting alone is not enough. Although the FBI received a tip giving them "information about Cruz's gun ownership, desire to

KNIVES ARE NOT THE SAME

"A series of ... knife attacks on schools in China in 2010–2012 resulted in many dead and wounded, but never more than ten and frequently with no fatalities at all."

–Gavin Magrath, lawyer and *Huffington Post* contributor

Gavin Magrath, "For 2013, Let's Ban Cars and Guns," *Huffington Post*, last updated March 5, 2013. www.huffingtonpost.com/gavin-magrath/gun-control-debate_b_2389047.html.

kill people, erratic [unpredictable] behavior, and disturbing social media posts, as well as the potential of him conducting a school shooting,"[27] the matter was not investigated. After the shooting, the FBI admitted that "established protocols ... were not followed. The information was not provided to the Miami Field Office, and no further investigation was conducted at that time."[28] This is a clear example of the importance of training for law enforcement officials and of establishing—and following—guidelines to help them identify and investigate true threats.

Addressing the Issue of Suicide

While women suffer more from gun violence in an abusive relationship, the danger to men when there is a gun in the house comes more often from themselves. Research has shown that women account for about 14 percent of gun suicides; men, on the other hand, represent an alarming 86 percent. Among people between the ages of 15 and 19, the second leading cause of death is suicide, and numerous studies have shown that people who attempt suicide with a gun complete their attempt more often than people who attempt suicide using any other method. Additionally, suicide is the cause of nearly twice as many gun deaths as homicide in the United States.

The presence of a gun does not make a person want to commit suicide, but a person with suicidal thoughts who knows a gun is accessible may make a sudden decision to use it. Other methods of suicide, such as taking a lethal dose of pills, take at least a few moments of time and planning that allow the person to consider what they are about to do and perhaps seek help. A gun that is readily available at home requires no planning and is an instantaneous way to end one's life.

For several reasons, suicide with a firearm is an especially high risk for people who have served in the military, the most obvious being that the military gives them guns, so they are always present. Combined with a mental illness such as post-traumatic stress disorder (PTSD), this easy access to guns increases the danger that someone may attempt suicide.

According to the Office of Suicide Prevention, in 2016, veterans accounted for 8.5 percent of the U.S. population but 18 percent of all adult suicides in the country.

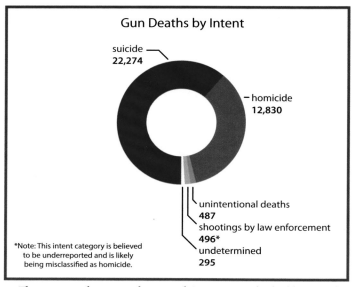

Gun Deaths by Intent

suicide — 22,274

homicide 12,830

unintentional deaths 487
shootings by law enforcement 496*
undetermined 295

*Note: This intent category is believed to be underreported and is likely being misclassified as homicide.

The gun suicide rate in the United States is nearly double that of the gun homicide rate, as this information from Everytown for Gun Safety shows. According to the organization, due to Americans' ease of access to guns, the country's gun suicide rate is eight times higher than that of other high-income countries.

Gun rights advocates tend to argue that without access to a gun, someone would simply use a different method—and while this may be true in some cases, it is false in many others. For example, in 2006, Israel passed new laws requiring Israeli soldiers to store their weapons at the army barracks instead of at home so it was not as easy for them to access their weapons when they were off duty. This caused a 40 percent decline in suicides among off-duty soldiers. As writer Gavin Magrath pointed out, "they certainly could have chosen another way, but they didn't and are still alive."[29]

Even gun rights advocates are concerned about this issue, although they may disagree that the solution is to restrict access to guns. Instead, they may support better access to mental health services and increased awareness of the problem.

In 2018, Clark Aposhian, the leader of the Utah Sports Shooting Council, teamed up with public health expert Cathy Barber to create a suicide prevention class that everyone in Utah is required to take in order to receive a conceal-and-carry permit. Aposhian and Barber included tips for gun owners who are suicidal or for people who know a gun owner who is suicidal. For instance, storing guns at a friend's house until the person feels better is one way to put time between the suicidal thought and the opportunity to attempt suicide—or, at least, attempt suicide by this method. According to Barber, this time frame is the main thing that prevents many people from carrying out their plans.

CHANGE THE CULTURE, NOT THE LAW

"Gun owning families can bring down the rate of firearm suicides, and we can do it without a government mandate."

—Clark Aposhian, Utah Sports Shooting Council chair

Quoted in Claire Schaeffer-Duffy, "Advocates for Gun Rights, Public Health Team Up to Prevent Suicides," *National Catholic Reporter*, June 7, 2018. www.ncronline.org/news/people/advocates-gun-rights-public-health-team-prevent-suicides.

"It Was an Accident"

Having a loaded gun accessible at home is not only dangerous if a member of the household is suicidal. It also poses another serious danger, especially in a household with children. From 2006 to 2016, nearly 7,000 people died from unintentional firing of guns, according to the CDC, and anywhere from one-sixth to one-third of them were children. In 2014 alone, 2,549 children died by gunshot and an additional 13,576 had gun-related injuries.

Guns are a widespread and often glorified image in American culture, with movies, television shows, and even cartoons showing guns frequently. Children who see this kind of media recognize what guns looks like, how they are held, and what they are used for. However, most children are considered too young to be taught proper gun safety and instead are just told not to touch their parents' guns. Gun cabinets with locks are sold for this reason, but sometimes people forget to lock up their guns or simply do not believe it is necessary. In 2015, a study performed by the journal *Pediatrics* surveyed 3,949 people and found that two-thirds of parents with young children did not keep their guns locked up and unloaded when they were not being used. Another study, which was published in the *American Journal of Public Health*, found that only 44 percent of gun-owning Americans store their guns safely. If children who have played with guns or seen them on TV come across loaded weapons in their home or the home of a friend or acquaintance, they may falsely believe they know how to handle one, and the consequences can be devastating.

To gun control advocates, requiring people to either keep guns out of their homes or at least to keep them unloaded and locked away when not in use—especially if children live in the home—is a small and very reasonable price for Americans to pay in exchange for preventing suicides and accidental deaths. "Parents often do not realize how easily a child can access a gun that is not locked, and we too often hear about the tragic consequences,"[30] said O. Marion Burton, former president of the American Academy of Pediatrics.

Another reason why many gun control advocates support requiring guns to be locked up is that keeping them out in the open can make it easier for someone else to steal them. For instance, in 2012, a 22-year-old man stole an assault-style rifle and went on a shooting spree in an Oregon mall. In response, Oregon citizens began pushing for stricter regulations, including a bill that would require gun owners to keep their guns locked up when they are not being used and to report any lost or stolen gun to the police within 24 hours after the owner notices it is missing. People who violate either of these rules would be fined up to $2,000, depending on the circumstances of the case, and could be taken to court if the weapon they left unlocked is later used to injure someone.

As of April 2018, some states had less strict versions of these laws in place; for instance, 11 states require people to report their lost or stolen guns. Gun rights activists have pushed back on these laws, stating that it is their right as law-abiding gun owners to store their guns however they want. Some have cited fears of not being able to get to a gun quickly in the event of an emergency, such as a break-in. Kevin Starett, the leader of the Oregon Firearms Federation, said, "This is not how you solve the problem of people who use guns in a criminal fashion, by punishing people who don't use guns in a criminal fashion."[31] Supporters of safe-storage and lost-and-stolen reporting laws have responded by pointing out that a gun is a potentially deadly tool that should be stored safely when not in use just like any other tool, even one that is not naturally dangerous. For example, a curling iron is not a weapon, but people unplug and put it away after using it so it does not start a fire. Most gun control advocates want all gun owners to use this same type of care with their guns.

Gun Ownership Does Not Equal Safety

One of the reasons why some gun owners oppose safe-storage laws is because they say it would make it harder for them to use the gun as protection from dangerous intruders. For example, if someone were to break into their house, they would have to unlock the gun cabinet and load the gun. In the time they are doing that, they fear, someone could either rob them or shoot them before they get to their own gun.

Gun control advocates and statistics experts point out that this fear is out of proportion to the threat. Professor Harold Pollack, co-director of the University of Chicago's Crime Lab, explained,

> I had the Chicago police run the number on homicides. In 2011, precisely one homicide listed "burglary" as the motive. Nationwide, there are about 100 burglary-homicides every year. When you compare that to more than 18,000 gun suicides, the conclusions seem pretty obvious ...

Home protection provides a common, all-too-understandable motive to buy a gun. Few things are scarier than the possibility that some violent intruder will break in when you and your loved-ones are home …

Yet having guns around brings risks, too. Practically speaking, it's not the incredibly rare risk of mass homicide, but the everyday risks of injury, accident, domestic altercations [fights], and suicide. The relative risks matter. And the fact is: lethal home invasions and burglaries are incredibly rare. You might not think so, since dramatic cases stick in your mind and tend to receive disproportionate press coverage. These cases are rare nonetheless.[32]

Keeping a loaded gun handy in case of an intruder can also sometimes have tragic consequences. There have been many instances of people mistaking family members or neighbors for an intruder and shooting them, which would not happen if they had to take the time to unlock a gun cabinet and load a gun. For example, in April 2018, a Florida news outlet reported, "Allison Simmons went to the bathroom … and used

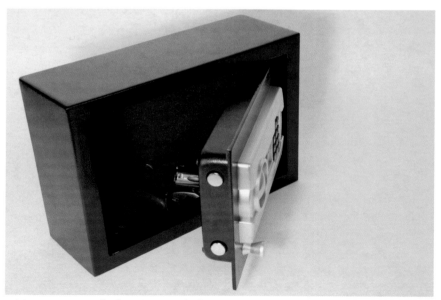

Many gun control advocates view locking gun cabinets or safes as a common-sense safety measure.

her cellphone for a flashlight … When she opened the [bedroom] door, Nathan Simmons thought she was an intruder and shot her twice, according to police."[33] Allison lived, but others have not been so lucky.

In addition, a gun is not always the most effective choice for fending off an intruder even if a home break-in does occur. Gun-safety training and shooting practice are not requirements for buying or owning a firearm—although many gun control advocates believe they should be, the same way driving lessons are required for owning a car—and a gun in the hands of an inexperienced user can actually pose a more serious threat to one's family than being unarmed. Bullets pass easily through walls, so a gun fired wildly in the direction of an intruder might miss its target but hit someone in another room. An unarmed home intruder could also manage to snatch a gun away and turn the homeowner's own weapon on them. As gun control supporters point out, it can be more dangerous to have a gun in one's home than not to have one at all. Laws prohibiting having weapons at home might actually save lives.

To Carry or Not to Carry?

Although suicides and accidental deaths due to guns are serious problems, many gun control activists are equally concerned about what can happen when people carry their guns around in public. Gun owners often wish to carry their weapons in public places for the same reason they want to have loaded guns at home—they want to be able to defend themselves if threatened. However, gun control advocates give some of the same arguments against carrying loaded guns as they do about having guns at home. Not everyone who carries a gun knows a lot about gun safety or has practiced with the weapon. An inexperienced shooter might fire in a panic and accidentally hit an innocent person standing nearby. A criminal attacker could also take the gun away from an inexperienced victim and use it on the victim or on bystanders. According to a 2009 study published in the *American Journal of Public Health*, a crime victim who carries a gun is

4.5 times more likely to be shot during an assault than a victim who does not carry a gun.

DOES THE GUN MAKE THE CRIMINAL?

"They (gun supporters) believe we need to shift attention to criminals, focus on the criminal, and they absolutely don't see the fact that the people who are committing most of the shootings and murders are not criminals until that moment."

—Pat Pascoe, former Colorado state senator

Quoted in Deborah Homsher, *Women & Guns: Politics and the Culture of Firearms in America.* Armonk, NY: Sharpe, 2002, p. 122.

Some states that allow citizens to carry guns require them to go through training in gun safety and how to handle one's weapon. However, this is not a universal requirement, which means that in some states, almost anyone over age 18 could be carrying a loaded weapon legally, even if they have received no training on how to use it safely. Even among states that do require training, some allow out-of-state visitors to carry their guns in public as long as they are licensed in their own state. This means that even in a state where training is required, some gun carriers are likely untrained.

Increasing the number of guns on the streets also increases the chance of accidents or the likelihood that a dispute over something trivial, such as a drunken argument in a bar or a road rage incident, could turn into a deadly shootout. Loose restrictions on gun ownership also make it easier for people to get their hands on weapons they can use to injure and kill many unsuspecting people in crowded areas in a matter of moments. Such tragedies happen every year in places such as schools, shopping malls, restaurants, parking lots, and movie theaters. Gun control activists disagree that armed bystanders could effectively halt such mass public shootings by firing at the shooter, which is one argument gun rights supporters often make.

One of the concerns people have about allowing people to get concealed carry permits with no training is that they may injure themselves with unsafe practices. Carrying a gun in a waistband, pocket, or anywhere aside from an easily accessible holster greatly increases the risk that someone will shoot themselves when they try to take their gun out.

Laws that allow people to own and carry guns may lead gun owners to use guns in self-defense in any situation where they feel threatened, even if a response such as walking away or talking through a misunderstanding would be more effective and sensible. There is also concern that some gun owners, believing in their right to form militias and protect themselves from government abuses, might form antigovernment groups and use firepower to threaten or strike out at government officials or agencies whenever they disagree with something the government does. Supporters of stricter gun control laws say it only makes sense that increasing the number of guns on the streets and in the hands of people will increase gun crime and the use of guns in situations that do not call for them, whereas limiting the carrying of guns in public and private places will logically lower the number of shootings around the nation.

THE ODDS ARE NOT GOOD

"The reality seems to be that when our bullets don't wind up in non-human animals or street signs, then when you use one to shoot someone, about 99 times out of … 100, you will commit a felony, shoot yourself, or shoot someone by accident. In one out of a hundred cases, you shoot the bad guy."

—Thomas T. Hills, professor of psychology at University of Warwick and author of *Statistical Life*

Thomas T. Hills, "The True Odds of Shooting a Bad Guy with a Gun," *Psychology Today*, January 12, 2017. www.psychologytoday.com/us/blog/statistical-life/201701/the-true-odds-shooting-bad-guy-gun.

Stricter Gun Laws Are Needed, Not Harsher Punishments

Gun control supporters argue that the high gun crime rate in the United States is evidence that stricter gun laws are needed, not more lenient concealed-carry policies. They compare the United States with other countries where guns are strictly controlled and murders and gun crimes are far less frequent. People on both sides of the debate often hold up Switzerland as a good example. Gun rights advocates point out that many people there own guns and are allowed to keep them at home, yet it has one of the lowest murder rates in the world. However, gun control advocates point out that this argument overlooks the fact that while Swiss citizens are indeed allowed to keep their guns at home, all ammunition must be kept in specific secure locations, such as a firing range or army barracks. They are also generally not allowed to carry guns in public. Additionally, gun training is a national tradition; for example, the country holds an annual shooting competition for teens between the ages of 13 and 17, so teens practice frequently. Prospective gun owners must pass a test to prove they know how to properly handle their weapon before they are issued a license. In addition, Switzerland has mandatory

A Good Guy with a Gun

One argument gun rights supporters commonly use is that public shootings could be stopped or prevented if people were allowed to carry guns in more places. This is frequently called the "good guy with a gun" argument because, its supporters say, a good guy with a gun who was on the scene of a mass shooting would be able to kill the shooter before they killed too many people. After the Parkland shooting, some people—including President Donald Trump—even suggested that school shootings could be prevented if teachers were allowed or required to carry guns. However, many people, including teachers themselves, believe that instead of decreasing the danger of school shootings, this act would increase it. As writer and teacher Annie Reneau pointed out, "Teachers are not soldiers or police officers or SWAT sharpshooters, and we shouldn't expect them to be … Soldiers and police train extensively to handle active shooter situations, both tactically and mentally. And even at that, trained law enforcement only have an 18% accuracy rate in high-stress shootout situations."[1]

Many incidents have disproven the "good guy with a gun" argument. For example, on November 22, 2018, shoppers in an Alabama mall were terrified after hearing gunshots. Outside, Emantic Fitzgerald Bradford Jr. also heard the gunshots. While people were fleeing the scene, he pulled out his own weapon and ran inside to try to defend the shoppers. An off-duty police officer who was working security at the mall saw Bradford holding the gun and killed him. The true gunman was never captured.

If police are looking for a gunman and they find someone with a gun, they do not always stop to check if they have the right person before they shoot. Bradford's lawyer suggested that the police officer was quicker to shoot because Bradford was black. Some argue that this is more of a race issue than a gun ownership issue, but since almost 60 percent of mass shooters are white men, it is possible that anyone who is not a uniformed law enforcement officer could be at risk of being mistaken for the shooter instead of being recognized as the "good guy." Additionally, the difficulty of hitting the right target in a high-stress situation with a lot of people running around greatly increases the danger of innocent people being shot as bullets go astray.

1. Annie Reneau, "Arming Teachers Is a Horrible Response to School Shootings, and This Is Why," *Scary Mommy*, accessed on January 9, 2019. www.scarymommy.com/arming-teachers-is-a-horrible-idea/.

military service for men, so most men are required to learn gun use and safety. Furthermore, although citizens are allowed to own guns, the authorities are strict about who is issued a permit. According to *Business Insider*, "They might consult a psychiatrist or talk with authorities in other cantons [regions] where a prospective gun buyer has lived before to vet the person."[34] Anyone who has been convicted of a crime, has a substance abuse problem, or has expressed a desire for violence is not allowed to buy a gun. However, even with all of these precautions, Switzerland has higher rates of gun violence and suicide by gun than other European countries where fewer people own guns.

People who oppose gun control often claim that the United States needs stricter punishment for criminals, not stricter laws to keep guns away from law-abiding citizens. However, since even more gun deaths result from suicides and accidents than criminal activities, gun control supporters insist that more gun laws and tighter controls are needed to keep American citizens safe. Also, stricter punishments for gun-related crimes have not, so far, proved to deter criminals from committing the crimes in the first place. "The question most offenders are asking is, am I going to get caught?" noted crime statistics researcher Don Weatherburn. "They're not sitting down and thinking, well if I am caught will I go to jail and if I do how long will I go for?"[35] Gun control supporters say keeping guns out of the hands of criminals in the first place will prevent more gun crimes than punishing criminals after they have already hurt someone.

Rejecting "Thoughts and Prayers"

Gun control activists are often accused of wanting to take away all guns from all citizens, but the majority of their arguments stress modifying existing gun laws to make them stricter in sensible ways rather than banishing guns from the United States altogether. They say, for example, that there is little logical reason to oppose policies such as waiting periods between buying a gun and taking it home, except by criminals or suicidal individuals who want to use their

What Is a Mass Shooting?

Mass shootings are one of the most high-profile issues in the gun control debate, but they are not well-defined, which leads to wildly varying numbers being tallied. The FBI uses the strictest definition: an incident where four or more victims, not including the shooter, are killed by gunshots. Using these criteria, there were at least 18 mass shootings in 2018, as of November of that year. Using the same criteria but counting people who were injured as well as killed, the Gun Violence Archive, a nonprofit organization that tracks gun violence in the United States, reported a total of 307 shootings in the same period of time. They took place in a variety of settings: in schools, bars, malls, a synagogue, and even a carwash. While some, such as the shooting in Parkland, Florida, received national attention, many did not, and there were other shootings that were not counted because only three people were killed or injured.

Some gun control groups argue that not counting injuries leads to a false tally. Jim Bueermann, president of the Police Foundation, an organization that researches law enforcement practices, said, "I would submit that sometimes the only difference between a shooting and a murder could be a centimeter, an inch, an unlikely ricochet, whatever."[1] On the other side of the argument, Mark Follman, an editor with the magazine *Mother Jones*, said that distinctions should be made between different types of violence because they often have different motivations and therefore different solutions. He said that including all shootings in which at least four people were injured "suggests that a 1 a.m. gang fight in a Sacramento [California] restaurant, in which two were killed and two injured, is the same kind of event as a deranged man walking into a community college classroom and massacring nine and injuring nine others."[2] The debate is likely to be ongoing and fierce, especially since each side tends to support the method of tallying that best supports their own arguments. Until an official definition is set, people should think critically about all mass shooting statistics.

1. Quoted in Chris Nichols, "How Is a 'Mass Shooting' Defined?," PolitiFact, October 4, 2017. www.politifact.com/california/article/2017/oct/04/mass-shooting-what-does-it-mean/.
2. Mark Follman, "How Many Mass Shootings Are There, Really?," *New York Times*, December 3, 2015. www.nytimes.com/2015/12/04/opinion/how-many-mass-shootings-are-there-really.html.

new purchase for a deadly purpose right away. "It's hard to understand why a person would need a gun immediately," said Richard Durbin, a former senator from Illinois who supported the Brady Act's gun control measures throughout the 1990s. "Bringing back the waiting period isn't about more government, it's about fewer gun crime victims."[36] Gun control activists argue that restrictions on guns, especially assault weapons and the ammunition for them, would only affect criminals, not law-abiding citizens who have no intention of assaulting anyone.

The goal of gun control is a safer America, an ideal its supporters say will be best achieved by reducing the number of deadly firearms in the nation and making it more difficult to obtain one. They believe that fewer guns in the hands of fewer people will logically translate to less gun crime and fewer gun suicides, and they point to regulations in other countries to back up their argument. As Magrath pointed out, "The U.S. is alone in its permissive attitude to guns among wealthy nations, and also alone in its gun ownership and gun killing rates."[37] To supporters of increased gun control in America, defending citizens from injuries and deaths caused by guns matters more than defending the centuries-old rules that allow people to have and carry them.

THOUGHTS AND PRAYERS DO NOT CREATE CHANGE

"It is positively infuriating that my colleagues in Congress are so afraid of the gun industry that they pretend there aren't public policy responses to this epidemic … There are, and the thoughts and prayers of politicians are cruelly hollow if they are paired with continued legislative indifference."

–Connecticut senator Chris Murphy

Quoted in AJ Willingham, "How 'Thoughts and Prayers' Went from Common Condolence to Cynical Meme," CNN, May 19, 2018. www.cnn.com/2018/02/20/us/thoughts-and-prayers-florida-school-shooting-trnd/index.html.

The fight for gun control has been ongoing for years, yet few changes have been made. Many citizens are fed up with the lack of government intervention and have begun to make their protests more visible. On March 24, 2018, thousands of Americans gathered across the nation to march for common-sense gun control. This demonstration, called the March for Our Lives, was organized by several student survivors of the Parkland shooting. They were outraged by the lack of government intervention after the massacre as well as by the things people were saying about gun violence. After every incident, politicians and others tend to make comments on social media about how their "thoughts and prayers" are with the victims and their families. Through merchandise and posters, the March for Our Lives organizers shared their message that "thoughts and prayers" were not enough. March for Our Lives has now become a nonprofit organization against gun violence, run by teenagers who were devastated but not destroyed by gun violence.

CHAPTER 4

The Gun Rights Side

The Declaration of Independence lists three inalienable rights: life, liberty, and the pursuit of happiness. Those rights serve as the foundation of the United States and are often used to justify controversial—and at times contradictory—topics. Gun rights lobbyists believe firearms are one way to ensure that citizens are able to defend those rights if anyone—including the government—tries to take them away. They argue that the authors of the U.S. Constitution and the Bill of Rights believed in an armed citizenry so much that they wrote it into law. Armed citizens cannot be easily overpowered by armed soldiers or police forces, whereas unarmed citizens can be. Corruption and governmental overreach were two of the primary

Many people see gun control proposals as useless at best and harmful to law-abiding citizens at worst.

motivations for the Founding Fathers to create the Constitution, and they believed a government that could be threatened by its citizens would be less likely to be corrupt.

The possibility that the United States could someday turn into what is called a police state, where the government secretly watches its citizens and controls them through a political police force, is one reason gun rights supporters cling tightly to their right to own firearms. Most supporters of gun rights believe that allowing citizens to own guns is essential to a free nation because it guarantees that a government will never easily be able to oppress its own citizens, no matter how powerful an organized national army may be. Many gun owners feel it is the public's responsibility to own guns as a safeguard against potential government oppression.

Supporters of gun ownership also believe guns equalize individual citizens. Those who may be physically smaller or weaker than a potential attacker have a much better chance at protecting themselves if they have a gun than if they face the assailant empty-handed. Many also feel that, since their right to own a gun is protected by the Constitution, any type of gun control is a restriction of their freedoms. Since the United States was founded on the principle of freedom, many gun rights supporters say that they are not required to have any reason for owning a gun other than wanting to do so. Some see it as a slippery slope to having other rights, such as the right to free speech or the right to vote, taken away or restricted.

Crime and Self-Defense

While gun control advocates generally believe making it harder to get guns will lead to a decrease in violence, gun rights activists disagree. In the first place, they say, other types of violent crime are likely to increase. They cite crime rates in countries with strict gun control to point out that banning or restricting guns has not eliminated all violence. Additionally, they frequently note that criminals do not have a problem breaking the law, including laws about who can have guns. They believe gun control laws would only reduce the ability of innocent victims to fight back against people who have obtained guns illegally.

Although guns are dangerous when used to commit crimes, they are also used in self-defense to stop crimes from happening. Statistics on the number of times guns are used for self-defense in the nation each year are debatable, since the definition of self-defense varies. Police reports are not always filed for incidents where no shots are fired, so polling gun owners is the way most of these statistics are obtained. Based on which researcher or organization conducts the poll and on which methods are used, the number of reported defensive gun uses ranges from 500,000 to more than 3 million incidents every year. The true number likely falls somewhere in the middle of this range.

Gun rights advocates frequently argue that gun control does not work because many criminals already get their weapons illegally—for instance, by buying them on the street.

Supporters of gun rights argue that the real crime would be to strip law-abiding citizens of a tool they might use for self-defense. After all, crimes happen suddenly, often in seconds, and generally when the criminal has made sure no one else is nearby who could help the victim. Even if a victim manages to call 911 during the course of a crime, various sources estimate that, on average, it takes between 7 and 18 minutes for police officers to respond to a call. This is often enough time for someone to commit a crime and leave the scene. Some also point out that while mass shootings happen more regularly in the United States than in other countries, the vast majority of U.S. gun owners will never be involved in any kind of gun violence—much less a mass shooting. Since mass shootings happen less frequently than other kinds of crime, even in America, gun rights advocates believe it does not make sense to legislate around this relatively rare occurrence.

Increasingly, people are deciding it is up to them to protect themselves. Gun lobbyists argue that every law-abiding American deserves the option to own a gun for that purpose. "Outside of criminology circles, relatively few people can reasonably estimate how often people use guns to fend off criminal attacks," noted gun use researchers Clayton E. Cramer and David Burnett. "If policymakers are truly interested in harm reduction, they should pause to consider how many crimes—murders, rapes, assaults, robberies—are thwarted each year by ordinary persons with guns."[38] In a nation where citizens are bombarded with news about violent crimes, many residents—especially those who live or work in high crime areas—arm themselves to feel safer from criminals.

Gun Control Does Not Work

Since the overwhelming majority of American gun owners do not commit crimes, laws forbidding people to keep or carry guns are seen by most gun rights activists as only punishing law-abiding citizens for the actions of criminals. Furthermore, many people say the gun control measures that do exist have

Accidental Shooting Is Not the Leading Cause of Death

Accidental shootings, especially of children, are one of the major reasons why people favor gun control. However, supporters of gun rights point out that the number of accidental deaths of children by firearms falls short of the number of children each year who accidentally drown. This is the leading cause of death for children ages one to four. According to the CDC, accidental death by firearm is the ninth leading cause of death for this age group, the eighth leading cause for children ages five to nine, and the tenth leading cause for children ages ten to fourteen. Any accidental death is tragic, but statistically, guns are not the deadliest danger to American kids. For this reason, some gun rights advocates say that if saving children's lives is the primary goal, then it might make more sense to ban swimming pools than to ban guns. Gun control advocates tend to counter this argument by pointing out that rather than banning either of these things, common-sense safety measures should be used around pools as well as guns. While they may not completely eliminate all risk of accidental injury or death, they can greatly reduce it.

Many gun rights advocates fully support measures to make guns safer and educate gun owners about safely using and storing their weapons, but they tend not to agree with the government passing laws requiring them to do so. Those who oppose these kinds of laws say it violates their freedom to do what they like with their own legally purchased possessions.

little effect on the number of gun-related crimes, since policies such as bans on assault-style weapons, background checks, and waiting periods only work for people who follow the law and obtain their weapons through licensed gun traders. Most criminals do not use legal channels to find their weapons in the first place.

Gun rights advocates offer many forms of proof that gun control policies do not work. For example, while many gun control advocates support raising the gun purchasing age from 18 to 21, gun rights advocates point out that people over 21 still commit crimes. They also claim that even if guns were restricted, violence would still occur. For instance, Australia banned certain types of guns after a mass shooting in 1996 and instituted stricter regulations on the types that were still legal. While the country's rates of gun violence and overall murder have fallen dramatically since then, its rates of other violent crimes, such as kidnapping and robbery, have not. In an article for the *Federalist*, attorney and former U.S. Army sniper team leader Ryan Cleckner wrote, "Completely eradicating gun violence wouldn't have stopped the 9/11 terrorist attacks, the Boston marathon bombing, the serial bombings in Austin, Texas, or other violent crimes."[39] Gun control advocates counter this point by arguing that the point of gun control is not to completely eliminate all violence; it is simply intended to make it more difficult for people to shoot themselves or others.

Cleckner also stated that violent crime has been dropping in the United States, while sales of AR-15 guns have increased. This type of gun, which, as of 2019, has been used in 11 mass shootings since 2012, has become especially controversial in recent years because although it is a semiautomatic rifle and can therefore only shoot one bullet at a time, it is highly accurate and easy to modify with accessories such as bump stocks. While it is true that violent crime and murder rates both fell in 2017—the first year since 2014 both rates had not risen—the ATF is not legally allowed to keep a national registry of assault rifle sales, so it is difficult to prove or disprove Cleckner's argument that there are more AR-15s in circulation today. Dave Chipman, a former ATF employee and current senior policy advisor at the Giffords Law Center to Prevent Gun Violence, "estimated that there are 10 million assault rifles currently in circulation, but he said he had 'no comfort level' with that number ... 'Even if that's right, is it 10 people with a million guns, or 10 million people with one gun? We don't know, and that doesn't help good govern-ment looking out for public safety."[40] The NRA and many gun rights advocates oppose a national gun registry out of fear that if the government knows who has guns, it will be easy for them to target those gun owners, either with laws or by physically taking away their guns.

The AR-15 (shown here) has been the source of particularly contentious debate.

Another reason gun rights advocates say gun control does not work is because statistics from the United States show that stricter gun laws do not necessarily correlate with less gun crime. Statistics from the State Firearm Laws project and the Gun Violence Archive show that states that have less restrictive gun laws, such as Vermont, North Dakota, and Wyoming, have some of the lowest gun homicide rates. However, other states, such as California, Maryland, and Illinois, have strict gun control laws but high rates of gun homicide. An editorial column by the *Washington Examiner* stated, "Texas and California have comparable gun homicide rates each year ... If gun control were effective, this is not what you'd expect in the nation's two most populous states with two of the most different gun policies."[41] While this is true, it is not the whole picture. First, gun control advocates are concerned with more than just the number of gun murders; they also want to decrease gun suicides and accidents. When all gun deaths are compared, not just gun murders, stricter gun control generally correlates to lower rates of gun deaths, according to research published in *Fortune* magazine.

California has about 10 million more residents than Texas. When the gun deaths are averaged out among the populations, California has a lower rate of gun deaths than Texas—according to the CDC, in 2017, these rates were 7.9 and 12.4 respectively, making Texas's rate higher than the national average of 11.8. Even if guns are not outright banned, imposing restrictions such as safe storage laws has been shown to decrease the number of gun deaths.

Second, California and Illinois are unique because some of their cities have high rates of gang violence. Gun ownership and shootouts among gangs disproportionately increase these states' gun homicide rates, which contributes to an increase in the overall rate of gun deaths. Third, some states with strict gun control laws are bordered by states with loose ones. Therefore, while it may be difficult to legally or illegally obtain a gun in a state with strict laws, it may be easier to do so in a bordering state and take it back over the border unnoticed. As Magrath pointed out, examples of failed gun control in specific states such as Illinois and California "do not show … that gun control in the U.S. does not work. What they do show is that attempting to regulate locally … will never be effective: coordinated national efforts are required."[42]

Strengthen Existing Laws Instead of Making New Ones

One thing gun rights and gun control advocates agree on is that all the laws in the world will not make a difference if they are not effectively enforced. The Gun Control Act of 1968 restricts who can own a gun, but sometimes people on that list end up being able to buy guns legally anyway because

MOST GUN OWNERS SUPPORT REGULATION

"It's a myth that gun owners despise regulation. Instead, they tend to believe that government regulation should have two purposes—deny guns to the dangerous while protecting rights of access for the law-abiding."

—David French, military veteran and gun owner

David French, "What Critics Don't Understand About Gun Culture," *The Atlantic*, February 27, 2018. www.theatlantic.com/politics/archive/2018/02/gun-culture/554351/.

the system that is supposed to flag them is faulty in some way. For example, in 2007, a man named Seung-Hui Cho legally bought a gun and then went on to kill 33 people and then himself in a shooting spree at the Virginia Polytechnic Institute and State University, often shortened simply to Virginia Tech. An investigation into the incident revealed that Cho had been found "mentally ill and in need of hospital-ization" and "an imminent danger to self and others"[43] in a court-ordered mental health evaluation in December 2005. However, because the court decided he could receive out-patient care (seeing a therapist regularly while living in his own home) instead of inpatient (being admitted to a mental health facility), he was not considered by the state of Virginia to fit the legal definition of a mental defective, which, under the 1968 act, would have barred him from buying a gun. His background check came up clean, causing many people, such as Kristin Rand of the Violence Policy Center, to criticize the narrowness of Virginia's law.

The *Washington Examiner* suggested,

Congress should at least consider granting money to the states to pay for the personnel and computer resources required to make the background check database work as intended. Mean-while, it should also consider creating a universally accessible, voluntary background check system ... to replace or supplement the National Instant Criminal Background Check System.

The next step will likely fall to state governments, which may want to consider new ideas such as temporary gun violence restraining orders. They probably also ought to be reconsidering procedures for officially identifying and legally recognizing mental illness in people who are suspected threats to themselves and others.[44]

Some agree with these measures, while others believe they could have negative effects on mentally ill people while having no effect on gun crime. Many mental illnesses do not cause someone to be a danger to themselves or others, and many people who should be barred from having a gun never seek mental health counseling, so their background check would not be flagged.

Furthermore, experts have noted that most people who commit gun crimes do not have any mental illness; in fact, people with mental illnesses are generally more likely to be the victims of violence than the perpetrators. Some gun rights activists say that instead of creating new laws that could unnecessarily ban certain people from having guns, the

COULD A GUN HAVE PREVENTED A TRAGEDY?

"Speaking for myself, I would give anything if someone on campus; a professor, one of the trained military or guardsman taking classes or another student could have saved my daughter by shooting Cho before he killed our loved ones."

—Holly Adams, mother of a victim of the 2007 Virginia Tech shooting

Quoted in "A VT Victim's Parent Speaks Out AGAINST Gun Control," Virginia Citizens Defense League, April 16, 2012. www2.vcdl.org/webapps/vcdl/vadetail.html?RECID=6619361.

government should focus on giving citizens better access to quality, affordable mental health care.

Stamping Out Gun Crime

In 2007, California passed a law requiring all newly manufactured handguns to have microstamping technology. Whenever a gun is shot, a firing pin strikes the bullet casing—a shell containing gunpowder and the bullet. Microstamping puts a unique mark on the firing pin so it leaves a specific imprint on every bullet fired out of the gun. The technology makes it possible for police to potentially trace bullets back to the precise handgun that fired them—and to the owner of that gun. Gun rights activists resist the idea of microstamping, however, viewing it as a way for the state to decrease the number of handguns available without actually banning them. When the rule was passed, handgun manufacturer Smith & Wesson decided to stop making new handguns available in California because, according to a press release by the company, "a number of studies have indicated that microstamping is unreliable, serves no safety purpose, is cost prohibitive and, most importantly, is not proven to aid in preventing or solving crimes."[1]

1. Quoted in "Mission Impossible: California Court Upholds Microstamping Law," NRA Institute for Legislative Action, July 3, 2018. www.nraila.org/articles/20180703/ mission-impossible-california-court-upholds-microstamping-law.

Common Sense Without Gun Control

Except for those on the fringes of both sides of this issue, gun rights and gun control supporters alike support what many people call common-sense restrictions. It makes sense, for example, to require gun owners to register their weapons with the government. After all, a driver's license is required for a person to legally operate a vehicle, so having similar restrictions on owning a potentially deadly weapon does not seem unreasonable. Most gun owners believe a person who owns a gun should know how to use it; they know better than anyone how much damage a gun can do in untrained hands. Just as most gun control advocates seek reasonable restrictions on gun ownership rather than the complete ban of all guns in America, most gun rights activists are willing to consider certain policies that restrict gun ownership.

Nevertheless, gun lobbyists are often accused of being stubborn in their opposition to gun control. For example, they typically oppose waiting periods between the time a gun is purchased and the time the buyer is allowed to take it home. They point out that waiting periods can, in fact, harm people who fear for their life and want a gun immediately for self-defense. A woman who has recently left an abusive husband or boyfriend, for example, might fear he will attack her and buy a gun to protect herself. A waiting period could keep her from taking the weapon home for several days, and during that time, she might be attacked or even killed by the man. Gun rights advocates cite instances where such situations have occurred to point out that there are reasons to want a gun right away that have nothing to do with wanting to commit a crime. Many gun rights supporters oppose waiting periods as needless examples of government control that might harm law-abiding gun buyers but do little to avert gun sales to the many criminals who get their guns through channels that require no waiting period anyway.

An American Freedom

Gun lobbyists passionately defend their right to keep and bear arms and oppose many suggested measures by the government to infringe on this right. They do not see gun control as having anything but a worsening effect on crime in the United States, and they point out that the overwhelming majority of guns and gun owners are law-abiding citizens whose guns are never used in a crime. At best, gun rights supporters perceive any government effort to control firearms as misinterpreting gun statistics and taking away an important American freedom when there is no proof that doing so will reduce crime. At worst, gun lobbyists see gun control as a government effort to control American citizens by removing their ability to stand up for themselves if the government ever becomes corrupt and turns on its people.

Supporters of guns and the Second Amendment are typically suspicious of any proposed law that could threaten or diminish gun ownership among the law-abiding people of America. Americans, they say, should have the choice of whether or not to carry a gun, rather than having the government make that choice for them. "Gun advocates favor freedom, choice and self-responsibility," said journalist John Stossel. "If someone wishes to be prepared to defend himself, he should be free to do so. No one has the right to deprive others of the means of effective self-defense, like a handgun."[45]

CHAPTER 5

The Debate Is Ongoing

There are many factors that come into play when it comes to gun ownership in America. Researchers from all over the world have conducted surveys, collected statistics and anecdotal evidence, and performed studies on the topic. The same results are often used to support contradictory arguments, making it difficult to determine anything concretely. For example, a study on the number of people killed by guns each year may be used to argue that guns are deadly and should be banned but also to argue that guns are less deadly than many other things, such as cars and poisonous substances. Those who seek tighter gun restrictions collect data and cite studies supporting arguments about gun violence, accidents, and reckless gun ownership. Those who seek fewer laws regulating gun possession collect data and cite studies in support of gun use for self-defense, gun-related sports, and responsible gun ownership.

The media adds to the dispute. Every time there is a mass shooting, national media coverage is intense and often lasts for weeks, creating a surge of sympathy and outrage. Typically, people on one side of the debate call for better gun control after a shooting, which prompts people on the other side of the debate to buy more guns out of fear that new measures will pass and prevent them from doing so.

The presence of guns is not the only factor that affects crime; geography, social class, and other factors also play a role. Adding to the controversy is the fact that gun control has been used in the United States as a means to disarm people of color and those who live in poverty. However, people of color are statistically more likely to die from injuries resulting from firearms than white Americans.

DIFFICULT QUESTIONS

"One thing there is consensus on is guns increase the lethality of violence. There's less agreement on whether guns lead to more violence or less ... It's a very difficult question to answer with scientific certainty."

–Daniel Webster, co-director of the Johns Hopkins Center for Gun Policy and Research

Quoted in Ronald J. Hansen and Dennis Wagner, "Guns in Arizona: A Life-or-Death Question," *Arizona Republic*, July 17, 2011. archive.azcentral.com/arizonarepublic/news/articles/2011/07/17/20110717 arizona-guns-special-report-life-or-death-question.html.

Guns and Geography

America's endless gun debate has a great deal to do with geography. The United States is a large nation with many big cities but also sweeping rural areas. Cities are by far the most likely places in the nation for innocent people to be shot. Crime rates vary from city to city and even from area to area within a city, but the CDC reports that more than 50 percent of all gun homicides in the United States happen in the 50 largest metropolitan areas. Inner-city residents especially tend to support laws that would let fewer people have guns, since their risk of being shot is twice the national average. However, other people who live in cities support gun rights for exactly this reason: They feel unsafe and want to be able to protect themselves in the event that they encounter an armed criminal.

Rural communities, on the other hand, have relatively low crime and murder rates. This is partly because they are not as densely populated—where there are fewer people, there are generally fewer crimes. However, even the per capita crime rate—which adjusts for population density by counting the number of crimes that happen per thousand or hundred thousand residents—tends to be much lower in the country than in the city. Many people in the country also enjoy using their guns to hunt or find them fun to shoot at inanimate targets, and there are fewer indoor shooting ranges in rural areas where someone would be able to go if keeping guns in the home was restricted. This is one reason why gun control tends to gain favor in cities but is unpopular in most rural areas.

Shooting guns for fun is a popular pastime in many rural areas where there is a much lower chance of accidentally hitting someone.

State or Federal Issue?

Gun control is not just about cities versus the country or liberals versus conservatives. It has also traditionally been part of a larger struggle between states and the federal government. Since the writing of the Constitution, Americans have disagreed about whether state governments or the federal government should have the most power. The initial 13 colonies had trouble coming together as a nation because some of them preferred to do things their own way and worried about federal power taking over. The American Civil War was, in essence, fought over the same issue—Southern states worried that the federal government would make a single law abolishing slavery throughout the country, so they broke away from the Union to protect their right to own slaves on their own terms.

To many Americans, leaving each state to create its own gun laws seems like the most logical choice. If Montana, a state with high gun ownership but very little gun crime, wishes to have lenient gun laws, many people say it should be allowed to do so; whereas if California, which has high gun crime rates, wishes to restrict guns, it, too, should be allowed to make the laws that best suit its needs. States do have a lot of freedom to pass their own gun laws, such as whether citizens are allowed to carry concealed weapons. However, some circumstances seem to require federal gun laws that apply equally to all states.

One example of a federal gun control law was the 1938 Federal Firearms Act that outlawed the purchase of a gun by any convicted felon anywhere in the country. If this law did not apply equally to all states, a felon might be able to obtain a gun in one state, then take it into another state that prohibited selling firearms to convicted felons. To make things fair, the federal government passed a single gun law that applied equally to all states. Regardless, taking guns across state lines remains a problem, prompting some people to suggest that state-governed gun control cannot work.

Not all Americans agree that tighter federal control of gun sales is the answer to America's gun and violence problems. The federal government is often seen as overstepping its bounds when it passes nationwide laws about things many people think states should decide for themselves, such as educational standards. Gun control, similarly, has become an important issue in the larger debate over whether states or the federal government should be in charge. This, too, divides Americans on their views of gun control. Some Americans see federal laws as an example of the government exerting too much power over states and people.

An Inefficient System

Although the ATF is meant to enforce existing gun control laws, it suffers from various setbacks that make it inefficient. Many of these are due to effective lobbying by the NRA. For instance, the organization has successfully lobbied to prevent the ATF from creating an electronic database that would allow officers to search through gun records by the buyer's name to trace the source of a gun that was used in a crime. When they need to review gun purchase records, they must go through millions of paper records by hand, which is time consuming and can lead to mistakes.

Another problem with the ATF is that it is understaffed, underfunded, and disadvantaged by certain laws. The agency is allowed—although not required—to inspect gun dealers to make sure they are following rules regarding proper background checks and keeping thorough records so guns can be traced if necessary. It is forbidden by law to inspect the same dealer more than once per year, but agents are so overworked that they generally cannot do even that. According to *McClatchy DC Bureau*, "In 2016, ATF inspected just 7.1 percent of 137,464 active firearms dealers for compliance. At that rate, it would take the agency 14 years to inspect all firearms dealers—likely longer, as the number of dealers has been steadily increasing."[1] This is unfortunate, because inspections generally reveal a number of dangerous mistakes or intentional violations:

> In fiscal year 2016, one-third of inspections found some sort of violation, the majority of which were serious; those include a dealer selling a firearm to someone they had reasonable cause to believe was prohibited, or failing to report multiple handgun sales to a single buyer ... Most violations tend to be due to "honest mistakes and carelessness" ... but if inspectors don't come in to tell sellers what they're doing wrong, the mistakes tend to continue ... Additionally, while educational resources for firearms dealers still exist, they've dropped off from what they were a decade ago and are not mandatory for those applying for a license to open shop.[2]

The ATF has requested additional resources for years, but as of 2019, Congress has yet to allocate more funds that would allow the agency to do its job more effectively.

1. Kate Irby, "With Resources Scarce, ATF Struggles to Inspect Gun Dealers," *McClatchy DC Bureau*, last updated January 9, 2018. www.mcclatchydc.com/news/nation-world/national/article193268134.html.

2. Irby, "With Resources Scarce, ATF Struggles."

Keeping the Peace

As gun control increasingly becomes a struggle between state and federal governments, it also becomes a fight among local, state, and federal police officers. When federal gun control laws are passed, such as the 1994 Brady Act's requirement to run background checks on anyone who wants to buy a gun, local police agencies must do most of the work of implementing it. This can increase the workload and paperwork burden on local police officers. "Under the Brady Act, state and local law enforcement officers had been forced to spend literally millions of hours investigating handgun buyers,"[46] said attorney and political science researcher David B. Kopel.

THE PROBLEM WITH POWER

"I don't think NRA members are bad people at all. I think they're responsible gun owners that want to become politically active and make their voices heard in this democracy ... I think the problem comes in when it's people at the top of this organization that don't listen to their constituents, and continue to scare people into buying more guns, creating more violence so they can scare more people and sell more guns."

–David Hogg, survivor of the Marjory Stoneman Douglas High School shooting

Quoted in Brett Samuels, "Parkland Students: NRA Has Been 'Basically Threatening Us,'" The Hill, March 19, 2018. thehill.com/blogs/blog-briefing-room/379118-parkland-students-nra-has-been-basically-threatening-us.

Local police also tend to favor gun rights for trained citizens because they realize they cannot prevent every crime from happening. In the average American community, there are only about 17 police officers for every 10,000 people, according to the FBI. This means that when a crime happens, it can take some time for police to get to the scene. Even a few minutes could make an important difference to someone's safety.

As the fear of mass shootings has increased, many local police forces now hold training drills to prepare to take on an active shooter while keeping innocent bystanders safe. Most civilian gun owners are not trained this way, but if police cannot get to the scene quickly, some argue that an armed civilian is better than nothing.

On the other hand, the increasing number of armed civilians on the streets does not always make a police officer's job easier. Some police officers also worry that an increase in armed citizens overall will lead to shootouts in situations where armed criminals otherwise might not have drawn their guns and fired. Additionally, not everyone who carries a gun is necessarily skilled at using it responsibly, especially in states with few to no training requirements for obtaining a concealed carry permit. Even if someone knows how to aim and shoot a gun, there may be things they were not taught to think about because not everyone is trained for a potential shootout situation. For instance, someone who is attempting to stop a criminal must think about what is behind the person before firing. Bullets can go right through a person, so if someone is standing behind the target, they could also be shot. Even if a "good guy with a gun" is at the scene, there may be times when they cannot safely shoot the

Guns and Schools

In 1990, Congress passed the Gun-Free School Zones Act to keep guns out of buildings and off the grounds of schools around the nation. Any adult caught carrying a weapon within half a mile of a school boundary faces possible jail time, and students caught on campus with a gun could be suspended or even expelled. The Gun-Free School Zones Act seemed to supporters like a sensible law to protect children and teenagers from guns. However, as with any gun control measure, it was met with controversy. States and communities questioned the federal government's ability to mandate that they follow the new policy, and the Supreme Court decided the requirement was unconstitutional. Today, states are allowed to create their own policies. Most follow some version of the act, but many gun rights activists say gun-free zones only encourage shooters. As Ryan Cleckner said, "It is logical that these monsters prefer unarmed victims."[1] Gun rights activists tend to believe that gun-free zones should be abolished, while gun control activists tend to believe the presence of guns in certain places, such as schools, would increase the danger to the people who have to be there every day.

Gun-free zones are a hotly debated topic.

1. Ryan Cleckner, "10 Common Arguments for Gun Control, Debunked," *Federalist*, March 21, 2018. thefederalist.com/2018/03/21/10-common-arguments-gun-control-debunked/.

criminal without injuring or killing innocent people, and accurately assessing all of these little details quickly in a high-stress situation is something most people are not trained to do.

An Emotional Debate

Americans have always had a unique relationship with guns, but support tends to increase when crime does, since having a gun for protection can make citizens feel safer. However, the Pew Research Center found that most Americans do not have an accurate perception of crime rates. Although violent crime has been decreasing steadily since 1993, aside from two spikes (one between 2004 and 2006, the other between 2014 and 2016), the organization's opinion surveys "regularly find that Americans believe crime is up nationally, even when the data show it is down."[47] This false belief that the country is getting more violent may contribute both to more support for guns and to more support for gun control, depending on each person's views.

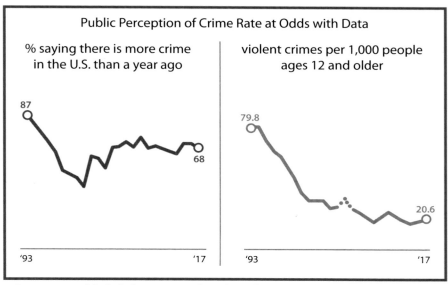

Contrary to public belief, crime rates have been decreasing relatively steadily for more than 20 years, as this information from the Pew Research Center shows.

Whether or not people have easy access to guns seems to have little impact on the nation's crime rates, despite the insistence of gun control advocates that more guns will equal more crime and the argument of the gun rights lobby that more guns will reduce crime. Nevertheless, people who favor gun control continue to fight for the stricter gun laws they feel will make the nation safer—preventing not just crime, but accidents and suicides as well—while gun rights supporters continue to fight for fewer restrictions on their right to keep firearms for sport, for self-defense, or simply because the Constitution says they can. "The gun issue has been, and will continue to be, one of the nation's most controversial and intractable policy issues,"[48] Robert J. Spitzer said.

THE BEST OF BOTH WORLDS

"Our nation does not have to choose between reducing gun-violence injuries and safeguarding gun ownership. Indeed, scientific research helped reduce the motor vehicle death rate in the United States and save hundreds of thousands of lives—all without getting rid of cars."

—Mark Rosenberg, former CDC gun violence researcher, and Jay Dickey, former Arkansas congressman

Quoted in Doug Irving, "More Research Could Help Prevent Gun Violence in America," RAND Corporation, July 10, 2018. www.rand.org/blog/rand-review/2018/07/more-research-could-help-prevent-gun-violence-in-america.html.

Gun control is an emotionally charged issue with no clear solution, and while people on both sides of the issue tend to want the same things—keeping Americans safe while upholding their rights as citizens—they disagree about the best way to go about it. Powerful lobbying groups further split the nation's opinions. Experts say more nonbiased research into gun violence is necessary to create useful gun control policies. The RAND Corporation, a research and analysis organization, studied gun policy in the United States over the course of two years and found that not enough research had been done to say for sure which policies would work best. This is mainly because, in 1996, the NRA successfully lobbied Congress to pass the

Dickey Amendment, which banned the CDC from doing research on gun violence. Jay Dickey, the sponsor of the bill, later withdrew his support from it, but the amendment is still in effect as of 2019. According to RAND,

> That has left mostly private foundations and universities to search for evidence about what works and what doesn't to prevent gun violence. Without government support, they also work without much government data. Researchers wanting to follow trends in gun ownership rates, for example, have had to try to estimate those numbers from hunting permits, firearm suicide rates, and even subscriptions to Guns & Ammo magazine.[49]

To try to fill this gap, RAND sponsored its own study, reviewing "thousands of books, journal articles, and research papers on gun policies and gun violence prevention."[50] The researchers found that most of the studies that had already been done did not meet the proper scientific standards to show a clear result based on a particular policy. Essentially, the only thing that is clear about the gun debate as of 2019 is that experts do not know enough about the issue to make effective policy changes. Until more research is done, it is likely the debate will stay as controversial as ever.

Introduction: The Parkland Massacre

1. Quoted in Emanuella Gringberg and Eric Levenson, "At Least 17 Dead in Florida School Shooting, Law Enforcement Says," CNN, February 14, 2018. www.cnn.com/2018/02/14/us/florida-high-school-shooting/index.html.

2. Quoted in Paula McMahon, Tonya Alanez, and Lisa J. Huriash, "Parkland Shooter Nikolas Cruz During Confession: 'Kill Me,'" *South Florida SunSentinel*, August 6, 2018. www.sun-sentinel.com/local/broward/parkland/florida-school-shooting/fl-florida-school-shooting-nikolas-cruz-confession-20180806-story.html.

Chapter 1: America's History with Firearms

3. Gregg Lee Carter, *Guns in American Society: An Encyclopedia of History, Politics, Culture and the Law*. Santa Barbara, CA: ABC-CLIO, 2002, pp. 85-86.

4. Quoted in Paul Halsall, "The Bill of Rights, 1689," Fordham University, August 1997. www.fordham.edu/halsall/mod/1689billofrights.asp.

5. U.S. Const. amend. II.

6. Robert J. Spitzer, *Gun Control: A Documentary and Reference Guide*. Westport, CT: Greenwood Press, 2009, p. xxiv.

7. James B. Jacobs, *Can Gun Control Work?*. New York, NY: Oxford University Press, 2002, p. 20.

8. Harry L. Wilson, *Guns, Gun Control, and Elections: The Politics and Policy of Firearms*. Lanham, MD: Rowman & Littlefield, 2007, p. 11.

9. Duncan Watts, *Dictionary of American Government and Politics*. Edinburgh, UK: Edinburgh University Press, 2010, p. 133.

10. Kristin A. Goss, *Disarmed: The Missing Movement for Gun Control in America*. Princeton, NJ: Princeton University Press, 2006, p. 39.

11. Quoted in Stephen A. Holmes, "Gun Control Bill Backed by Reagan in Appeal to Bush," *New York Times*, March 29, 1991. www.nytimes.com/1991/03/29/us/gun-control-bill-backed-by-reagan-in-appeal-to-bush.html?pagewanted=all&src=pm.

12. Quoted in "Brady Law Fails to Reduce Murders," United Press International, August 2, 2000. archive.newsmax.com/articles/?a=2000/8/1/183258.

Chapter 2: Guns and the Law

13. Benedict D. LaRosa, "The Second Amendment Protects an Individual Right," Future of Freedom Foundation, January 1, 2001. www.fff.org/explore-freedom/article/amendment-protects-individual/.

14. Patrick J. Charles, *The Second Amendment: The Intent and Its Interpretation by the States and the Supreme Court*. Jefferson, NC: McFarland, 2009, p. 23.

15. Quoted in Steve Chapman, "Column: Why the Second Amendment Is Irrelevant," *Chicago Tribune*, February 23, 2018. www.chicagotribune.com/news/opinion/chapman/ct-perspec-chapman-second-amendment-20180223-story.html.

16. Earl E. Pollack, *The Supreme Court and American Democracy: Case Studies on Judicial Review and Public Policy*. Westport, CT: Greenwood Press, 2009, p. 374.

17. Quoted in "Heated Debate over Assault Weapons," CBS, July 26, 2009. www.cbsnews.com/news/heated-debate-over-assault-weapons/.

18. Quoted in "Liberals Scramble to Extend Clinton Gun Ban," NRA Institute for Legislative Action, September 8, 2004. www.nraila.org/articles/20040908/liberals-scramble-to-extend-clinton-gun.

19. Sarah Thompson, "Raging Against Self Defense: A Psychiatrist Examines the Anti-Gun Mentality," Jews for the Preservation of Firearms Ownership, 2000. jpfo.org/filegen-n-z/ragingagainstselfdefense.htm.

20. Spitzer, *Gun Control*, p. 67.

21. Thad Morgan, "The NRA Supported Gun Control When Black Panthers Had the Weapons," History.com, March 22, 2018. www.history.com/news/black-panthers-gun-control-nra-support-mulford-act.

22. Fred E. Foldvary, "Concealed Weapons," *Progress Report*, 1999. www.progress.org/fold111.htm.

23. Robert McClelland, "New Gun and Ammo Taxes Sound Like Promising Ways To Reduce Gun Violence. But There Are Problems," *TaxVox*, May 24, 2018. www.taxpolicycenter.org/taxvox/new-gun-and-ammo-taxes-sound-promising-ways-reduce-gun-violence-there-are-problems.

Chapter 3: The Gun Control Side

24. German Lopez, "America Is One of 6 Countries that Make Up More than Half of Gun Deaths Worldwide," Vox, August 29, 2018. www.vox.com/2018/8/29/17792776/us-gun-deaths-global.

25. "Domestic Violence & Firearms," Giffords Law Center to Prevent Gun Violence, accessed on January 3, 2019. lawcenter.giffords.org/gun-laws/policy-areas/who-can-have-a-gun/domestic-violence-firearms/.

26. "Students at the Forefront: 'Boyfriend Loophole' with New Gun Law in Oregon," Break the Cycle, accessed on June 17, 2018. www.breakthecycle.org/blog/students-forefront-%E2%80%9Cboyfriend-loophole%E2%80%9D-closed-new-gun-law-oregon.

27. Quoted in Gabrielle Bluestone, "All the Times Nikolas Cruz Was Reported to Authorities Before the Florida Shooting," Vice News, February 16, 2018. news.vice.com/en_us/article/3k7vej/all-the-times-nikolas-cruz-was-reported-to-authorities-before-the-florida-shooting.

28. Quoted in Bluestone, "All the Times Nikolas Cruz Was Reported."

29. Gavin Magrath, "For 2013, Let's Ban Cars and Guns," *Huffington Post*, last updated March 5, 2013. www.huffington-post.com/gavin-magrath/gun-control-debate_b_2389047.html.

30. Quoted in Bonnie Rochman, "A Florida Judge Says It's O.K. for Pediatricians to Ask About Guns," *TIME*, September 15, 2011. healthland.time.com/2011/09/15/why-its-now-okay-for-pediatricians-in-florida-to-talk-about-guns/.

31. Quoted in Brian Freskos, "The Next Big Gun Controversy Is Forcing People to Lock Them Up," Vice, April 16, 2018. www.vice.com/en_us/article/xw7mnj/the-next-big-gun-controversy-is-forcing-people-to-lock-them-up.

32. Quoted in Ta-Nehisi Coates, "Gun Violence and the Irrational Fear of Home Intrustion," *The Atlantic*, December 23, 2012. www.theatlantic.com/national/archive/2012/12/gun-violence-and-the-irrational-fear-of-home-invasion/266613/.

33. Monique Valdes and Megan Cruz, "Man Mistakes Wife for Intruder, Shoots Twice as She Returns from Bathroom, Police Say," WFTV9, April 26, 2018. www.wftv.com/news/local/police-man-shoots-wife-twice-thinking-shes-intruder-/738959606.

34. Hilary Brueck, "Switzerland Has a Stunningly High Rate of Gun Ownership—Here's Why It Doesn't Have Mass Shootings," *Business Insider*, December 11, 2018. www.businessinsider.com/switzerland-gun-laws-rates-of-gun-deaths-2018-2.

35. Quoted in Liz Foschia, "Tough Prison Terms Don't Reduce Crime: NSW Study," Australian Broadcasting Corporation, March 12, 2012. www.abc.net.au/news/2012-03-13/tough-prison-terms-don27t-reduce-crime3a-study/3886402.

36. Quoted in "Lawmakers Introduce Bill to Permanently Re-instate Brady Waiting Period," Brady Campaign to Prevent Gun Violence, February 24, 1999. www.bradycampaign.org/media/press/view/164.

37. Magrath, "For 2013, Let's Ban Cars and Guns."

Chapter 4: The Gun Rights Side

38. Clayton E. Cramer and David Burnett, *Tough Targets: When Criminals Face Armed Resistance from Citizens*. Washington, DC: Cato Institute, 2012, p. i.

39. Ryan Cleckner, "10 Common Arguments for Gun Control, Debunked," *Federalist*, March 21, 2018. thefederalist.com/2018/03/21/10-common-arguments-gun-control-debunked/.

40. Kate Irby, "Nobody Knows Exactly How Many Assault Rifles Exist in the U.S.—by Design," *McClatchy DC Bureau*, February 23, 2018. www.mcclatchydc.com/news/nation-world/national/article201882739.html.

41. "Gun Control Is a Fantasy. Start a Realistic Conversation About Preventing School Massacres," *Washington Examiner*, February 21, 2018. www.washingtonexaminer.com/gun-control-is-a-fantasy-start-a-realistic-conversation-about-preventing-school-massacres.

42. Magrath, "For 2013, Let's Ban Cars and Guns."

43. Quoted in Jake Tapper and Avery Miller, "'Mentally Ill' but Still Able to Buy a Gun," ABC News, April 19, 2007. abcnews.go.com/WNT/VATech/story?id=3059185&page=1.

44. "Gun Control Is a Fantasy," *Washington Examiner*.

45. John Stossel, "Gun Control Isn't Crime Control," *New York Sun*, February 27, 2008. www.nysun.com/opinion/gun-control-isnt-crime-control/71908.

Chapter 5: The Debate Is Ongoing

46. David B. Kopel, "The Brady Bill Comes Due: The *Printz* Case and State Autonomy," *George Mason University Civil Rights Law Journal*, vol. 9, Summer 1999, p. 190. davekopel.org/2A/LawRev/BradyBillComesDue.htm.

47. John Gramlich, "5 Facts About Crime in the U.S.," Pew Research Center, January 3, 2019. www.pewresearch.org/fact-tank/2019/01/03/5-facts-about-crime-in-the-u-s/.

48. Quoted in Spitzer, *Gun Control*, p. xx.

49. Doug Irving, "More Research Could Help Prevent Gun Violence in America," RAND Corporation, July 10, 2018. www.rand.org/blog/rand-review/2018/07/more-research-could-help-prevent-gun-violence-in-america.html.

50. Irving, "More Research."

Chapter 1: America's History with Firearms

1. How did the Gun Control Act of 1968 differ from the National Firearms Act of 1934 and the Federal Firearms Act of 1938? Which do you think was most successful and why?

2. What are some similarities and differences between the government's prohibition of alcohol and its efforts to regulate gun ownership in America?

3. Guns and freedom are linked in American culture. Do you think it is possible to separate them? Why or why not?

Chapter 2: Guns and the Law

1. The Second Amendment is one of the most dissected sentences in the Constitution. What do you think the original authors intended? Support your answer.

2. What are some possible pros and cons of requiring background checks and waiting periods for gun purchases?

3. The author says gun rights activists see taxing ammunition as a sneaky form of gun control. Do you think ammunition taxes are ethical gun control measures, or are they underhanded? Explain your reasoning.

Chapter 3: The Gun Control Side

1. How do U.S. crime statistics compare with those of other developed countries? How do you think the presence of guns affects these statistics?

2. As technology continues to advance, there are more and more options for getting around gun control regulations in order to purchase a gun. Do you think it is possible for the government to adapt to things such as 3-D printed weapons? If so, how?

3. Do you think keeping a gun in the home makes the home safer or more dangerous for the people who live there? Why?

Chapter 4: The Gun Rights Side

1. In what ways do you think American citizens benefit from the right to bear arms?

2. If all guns were banned in the United States, what might the consequences be for law-abiding citizens? For criminals?

3. What do you think of the notion that the government wants to control American citizens by taking away their right to own weapons?

Chapter 5: The Debate Is Ongoing

1. Despite the historic lows of violent crime within the last decade, many Americans believe crime is more prevalent than it really is. Why do you think that is? Defend your opinion.

2. Imagine you were a police officer. Make an argument for or against laws to allow armed citizens in the public spaces of your community.

3. If a poll asked your opinion of the National Rifle Association (NRA), how would you answer and why?

Brady Campaign to Prevent Gun Violence

840 First Street NE, Suite 400
Washington, DC 20002
(202) 370-8100
www.bradycampaign.org

> As a leading organization against gun violence in America, the Brady Campaign works toward the goal of safety at home, at school, at work, and in communities. The organization works to pass and enforce sensible federal and state gun laws, regulations, and public policies by engaging in grassroots activism, electing public officials who support common sense gun laws, and increasing public awareness of gun violence.

Coalition to Stop Gun Violence (CSGV)

805 15th Street NW
Washington, DC 20005
(202) 408-0061
csgv@csgv.org
www.csgv.org

> The Coalition to Stop Gun Violence seeks to secure freedom from gun violence through research, strategic engagement, and effective policy advocacy.

National Rifle Association (NRA)

11250 Waples Mill Road
Fairfax, VA 22030
(800) 672-3888
www.nra.org

> Since 1871, the NRA has focused on firearms education and training for American citizens. Today, it is most widely recognized as a major political force, but it also holds training classes and seminars on a variety of topics, such as ways to avoid being targeted by criminals.

Second Amendment Foundation

12500 NE 10th Place

Bellevue, WA 98005

(425) 454-7012

info@saf.org

www.saf.org

> This nonprofit organization works to educate citizens about their Second Amendment rights and to bring lawsuits regarding gun rights to court.

Violence Policy Center (VPC)

1025 Connecticut Avenue NW, Suite 1210

Washington, DC 20036

(202) 822-8200

vpc.org

> The Violence Policy Center is a national nonprofit organization that works to stop gun-related death and injury through research, advocacy, education, and lawsuits. The center approaches gun violence as a public health issue, advocating that firearms be held to the same health and safety standards that all other consumer products must meet.

Books

Allen, John. *Gun Control*. San Diego, CA: ReferencePoint Press, 2018.
This book examines both sides of the gun debate.

Braun, Eric. *Never Again: The Parkland Shooting and the Teen Activists Leading a Movement*. Minneapolis, MN: Lerner Publications, 2019.
Increasingly, young adults are leading the discussion regarding gun control. This book tells the story of the tragedy that defined a modern movement.

Calabi, Silvio, Steve Helsley, and Roger Sanger. *The Gun Book for Boys*. Shooting Sportsman Books, 2012.
Although the title states that this book is for boys, it contains information for teens of any gender about gun safety, including how to properly hold, shoot, store, and carry a gun. Knowing the basics of gun safety is essential for anyone who wants to use one of these weapons for defense or recreation.

Orr, Tamra. *Tucson Shooting and Gun Control*. Ann Arbor, MI: Cherry Lake Publishing, 2018.
By examining the 2011 shooting of Representative Gabrielle Giffords, this book takes an in-depth look at a modern example of gun violence and the different ways it is viewed by people with varying opinions on gun control.

Wolny, Philip. *Gun Rights: Interpreting the Constitution*. New York, NY: Rosen Publishing, 2015.
Gun control laws have been fiercely debated in the context of what the U.S. Constitution allows. Understanding this document is essential to understanding the gun debate, and this book helps readers do that.

Websites

Bureau of Alcohol, Tobacco, Firearms and Explosives (ATF)
www.atf.gov

> This law enforcement agency works to protect the public with information, training, research, and technology. Its website includes information about current gun laws, statistics, and a page where people can submit anonymous tips regarding illegal activity they have personally witnessed.

Giffords Law Center to Prevent Gun Violence
lawcenter.giffords.org

> This website contains information about existing gun laws and what kind of culture and policy changes are necessary to make the country safer.

Open Secrets: Gun Rights vs. Gun Control
www.opensecrets.org/news/issues/guns

> This post on the *Open Secrets* blog discusses the politics of the gun debate. The blog is run by the Center for Responsive Politics, a nonpartisan, nonprofit organization that tracks which groups give politicians campaign donations and assesses whether that is affecting the way those politicians vote on important issues.

March for Our Lives
www.marchforourlives.com

> March for Our Lives is a nonprofit lobbying organization founded by survivors of the Marjory Stoneman Douglas High School shooting.

USA Carry
www.usacarry.com

> This website features an interactive map of the United States to help gun owners learn more about the permit laws in various U.S. states and territories. It also features information about insurance, training, and the latest gun-related news. Registered users can sign up for reminders about renewing their permits and post on forums to connect with other gun owners. Always ask a parent or guardian before participating in an online forum.

A

Adams, Holly, 73
alcohol, 14–15, 25
American Civil War, 16–17, 80
American Journal of Public Health, 52, 55
American Revolution, 12, 25
ammunition, 13, 18, 33, 41–42, 58, 62
Aposhian, Clark, 51
assassinations, 14, 16, 18–19, 21

B

background checks, 7, 21–24, 29, 32–33, 38–39, 41–42, 68, 72–73, 81–82
bans, 14–15, 17–18, 20, 24, 26, 28, 30–31, 33, 36–37, 40, 46, 66, 68–69, 71, 73, 75, 77, 87
Barber, Cathy, 51
Bill of Rights, 12–13, 27–28, 64
Black Panthers, 36
Bradford, Emantic Fitzgerald, Jr., 59
Brady, James, 21–22
Brady Campaign to Prevent Handgun Violence, 21, 24
Brady Handgun Violence Prevention Act, 22–24, 26, 62, 82
Brown Bess, 11
Bueermann, Jim, 61
bump stocks, 40, 69
Bureau of Alcohol, Tobacco, Firearms and Explosives (ATF), 25, 40, 69, 81

Burnett, David, 67
Burton, O. Marion, 52

C

California, 36–37, 40, 61, 70–71, 74, 80
cannons, 10
Carter, Gregg Lee, 11
Centers for Disease Control and Prevention (CDC), 41, 45, 51, 68, 71, 78, 87
Chapman, Steve, 30
Charles, Patrick J., 28
children, 7, 51–52, 68, 84
China, 10, 48
Chipman, Dave, 69
Cho, Seung-Hui, 72–73
cities, 10, 14, 16–17, 71, 78–79
civil rights movement, 16–18, 36
Cleckner, Ryan, 69, 84
Clinton, Bill, 22, 24, 26
concealed carry, 35–38, 57–58, 80, 83
Cook, Philip, 24
Cornell, Saul, 18
Cramer, Clayton E., 67
Cruz, Nikolas, 6–7, 40, 48

D

deaths, 20, 40, 43–44, 47, 49, 52, 55, 60, 62, 68, 71
democracy, 9, 82
Dickey, Jay, 86–87
District of Columbia v. Heller (2008), 30–31
domestic violence, 22, 47–48

E
Elmer, Bruce N., 20
English Bill of Rights, 11

F
Federal Assault Weapons Ban, 24, 26
Federal Bureau of Investigation (FBI), 20, 23, 34, 48–49, 61, 82
Federal Firearms Act, 15, 80
Feinstein, Dianne, 40
felonies, 19, 22, 58, 80
First Amendment, 29–30
Foldvary, Fred E., 38
Follman, Mark, 61
freedom, 9, 11–12, 27–28, 33, 65, 68, 75–76, 80
French, David, 72

G
Giffords Law Center to Prevent Gun Violence, 21, 24, 47, 69
González, Emma, 7
Goss, Kristin A., 20
Gun Control Act, 19–21, 26, 72
Gun-Free School Zones Act, 84
gunpowder, 10–11, 74
gun shows, 32, 42
guns, types of
    assault weapons, 24, 29, 31, 33, 35, 62
    handguns, 11, 14, 17–19, 21–22, 30–31, 33–35, 41, 74, 82
    muskets, 11
    rifles, 14, 18, 33, 35, 40, 52, 69–70
    shotguns, 18, 35–36
Gun Violence Prevention and Safe Communities Act, 41

H
Hills, Thomas T., 58
Hinckley, John, Jr., 21
Hogg, David, 7, 82
homicides, 16, 20, 24, 43, 45, 49–50, 53–54, 70–71, 78

I
injuries, 6, 21, 34, 40, 47, 51, 54, 57, 61–62, 68, 78, 86

J
Jacobs, James B., 14

K
Kashuv, Kyle, 8
Kasich, John, 26
Kennedy, John F., 18–19
Kennedy, Robert, 18–19
King, Martin Luther, Jr., 16, 18–19
Kopel, David B., 82
Ku Klux Klan (KKK), 17

L
LaPierre, Wayne, 28, 33

M
Magrath, Gavin, 46, 48, 50, 62, 71
March for Our Lives, 63
Marjory Stoneman Douglas High School shooting, 6–8, 28, 32, 40, 48, 59, 61, 63, 82
mass shootings, 6, 44–45, 47–48, 59, 61, 67, 69, 77, 83
McClelland, Robert, 42
mental illnesses, 20–21, 49, 73
microstamping, 74
militias, 12–13, 17, 28, 30, 57
Mulford Act, 36
Murphy, Chris, 62

N

National Firearms Act, 15, 29
National Rifle Association (NRA), 7, 17, 28–29, 33, 36, 40, 70, 81–82, 86

O

Onion, 43–45
open carry, 35–38
Oswald, Lee Harvey, 18–19

P

Parkland shooting. *See* Marjory Stoneman Douglas High School shooting
Pascoe, Pat, 56
police, 9, 21–22, 38–39, 41, 48, 52–53, 59, 64, 66–67, 74, 82–83
police state, 65
Pollack, Earl E., 30
Pollack, Harold, 53
Prohibition, 14–16, 25

R

RAND Corporation, 42, 86–87
Reagan, Ronald, 21–22, 36
Rendell, Ed, 33
Reneau, Annie, 59
Rosenberg, Mark, 86
Rosenthal, Andrew, 29
rural areas, 78–79

S

Scalia, Antonin, 13
Second Amendment, 8, 13, 17–18, 26–31, 41, 76
self-defense, 9, 11, 30, 33, 35, 38, 41, 57, 65–67, 75–77, 86

Spitzer, Robert J., 14, 36, 86
Starett, Kevin, 53
Stossel, John, 76
suicides, 23, 43, 49–55, 60, 62, 71, 86–87
Switzerland, 44, 58, 60

T

Texas, 69–71
Thompson, Sarah, 35
Thompson submachine gun (Tommy gun), 14
3-D printing, 39

U

United Kingdom (UK), 9, 44–45
United States v. Miller (1939), 29–30
U.S. Congress, 21–22, 26, 29, 33, 41, 62, 72, 81, 84, 86
U.S. Constitution, 12–13, 26, 28–29, 42, 64–65, 86
U.S. Supreme Court, 26, 29–31, 84

V

Vedantam, Shankar, 36
Virginia Tech shooting, 72–73

W

waiting periods, 7, 21–24, 60, 62, 68, 75
Washington Examiner, 70, 72
Weatherburn, Don, 60
Webster, Daniel, 78
Wild West, 13–14, 35–36
Wilson, Cody, 39
Wilson, Harry L., 15

PICTURE CREDITS

Cover DmyTo/Shutterstock.com; p. 7 Kevin Mazur/Getty Images for Time; p. 10 Oleg Proskurin/Shutterstock.com; p. 12 VCG Wilson/Corbis via Getty Images; p. 15 maumcerberwz/Shutterstock.com; pp. 16, 37 Bettmann/Bettmann/Getty Images; p. 19 © Corbis/Corbis via Getty Images; p. 22 Luke Frazza/AFP/Getty Images; p. 23 Guy J. Sagi/Shutterstock.com; p. 27 Emily Kask/AFP/Getty Images; p. 31 Robert Przybysz/Shutterstock.com; p. 39 Kelly West/AFP/Getty Images; p. 40 George Frey/Getty Images; p. 43 Erik McGregor/Pacific Press/LightRocket via Getty Images; p. 47 Jan Mika/Shutterstock.com; p. 54 Terry's Trails/Shutterstock.com; p. 57 Maksym Dykha/Shutterstock.com; p. 64 Gregory Johnston/Shutterstock.com; p. 66 Dragon Images/Shutterstock.com; p. 70 Ambrosia Studios/Shutterstock.com; p. 79 Alfred Wekelo/Shutterstock.com; p. 83 Stan Lim/Digital First Media/The Press-Enterprise via Getty Images; p. 84 Sascha Burkard/Shutterstock.com.

Lianna Tatman has a master's degree in cultural management. She has varied work and research experience. When it is not cripplingly cold, Lianna enjoys spending time outside with her dog, Hemingway. When it is cold, Lianna enjoys nothing.